STUDIES IN ENGLISH LITERATURE No. 34

General Editor
David Daiches
Dean of the School of English and American Studies
University of Sussex

BLAKE
The Lyric Poetry

by
John Holloway

EDWARD ARNOLD (PUBLISHERS) LTD.
41 Maddox Street, London W.1

© JOHN HOLLOWAY 1968

First published 1968

Boards edition SBN: 7131 5419 5
Paper edition SBN: 7131 5420 9

Printed in Great Britain by
The Camelot Press Ltd., London and Southampton

General Preface

It has become increasingly clear in recent years that what both the advanced Sixth Former and the university student need most by way of help in their literary studies are close critical analyses and evaluations of individual works. Generalizations about periods or authors, general chat about the Augustan Age or the Romantic Movement, have their uses; but often they provide merely the illusion of knowledge and understanding of literature. All too often students come up to the university under the impression that what is required of them in their English literature courses is the referring of particular works to the appropriate generalizations about the writer or his period. Without taking up the anti-historical position of some of the American 'New Critics', we can nevertheless recognize the need for critical studies that concentrate on the work of literary art rather than on its historical background or cultural movement.

The present series is therefore designed to provide studies of individual plays, novels and groups of poems and essays, which are known to be widely studied in Sixth Forms and in universities. The emphasis is on clarification and evaluation; biographical and historical facts, while they may, of course, be referred to as helpful to an understanding of particular elements in a writer's work, will be subordinated to critical discussion. What kind of work is this? What exactly goes on here? How good is this work, and why? These are the questions which each writer will try to answer.

DAVID DAICHES

Author's Preface

A great deal has been written about William Blake and his lyrics. But even when I have been most indebted to the work of others, I have felt that scholarship and criticism often over-weight the lyrics (as indeed the longer poems also) and hide their beauty and value. This book has been written in the conviction that when intricacies of discussion leave the reader with a less good, or even a less clearly good poem than he felt himself encountering at first reading, they are open to question and in fact probably wrong. I have also tried, within unavoidably strict limits of space, to bring out something of the symmetry and cogency of Blake's development as a lyric poet; and at the end, very briefly, to indicate his general place in English lyric verse, and how to study his lyric work is to find out something in general about the development of our literary culture.

I wish to express thanks to a number of my colleagues and students for discussion and information, and to Miss Joan Black for finding time to type much of the manuscript when it would otherwise have been delayed. I am also grateful, as always, for the help I have received from the staff of the Cambridge University Library.

JOHN HOLLOWAY

Wickhambrook

Contents

1. A Preliminary Review

In the course of this short book, I hope to show that Blake's lyrics were more immediately related to certain eighteenth-century traditions of thought and feeling than has been widely recognized; and moreover that this fact does not hide away from us the true poetic quality of what he wrote, but makes that quality all the plainer. This continuity with tradition, though, is not by any means with the eighteenth-century traditions that most readers call most readily to mind. A sensible first step is therefore to stress the newness of these poems, the fact that they make a break with their own time, a fresh start.

This was the point stressed by those who first published them: Blake's first poems, the *Poetical Sketches* of 1783, were published with a short *Advertisement*, written probably by the Rev. Henry Mathew. When Blake was growing up in his father's hosier's shop just off Golden Square (which is a stone's-throw from Piccadilly), Mathew was a preacher at St. Martin-in-the-Fields, and lived a short mile away in Charlotte street. He got to know Blake, and introduced him into the modest literary circle that visited at his house. Mathew's *Advertisement* does not, in fact, say overmuch for Blake's early lyrics, but it is precisely newness and freshness which (a little superciliously) it points to in them:

... they possessed a poetic *originality*, which merited some respite from oblivion.

This originality is what I hope to identify, at least in part, in the present chapter. The second chapter will re-open the matter of how, original as his lyrics were, Blake nevertheless had a place in certain traditions of writing in his time; and in the third chapter I shall bring these two points of view together, to show how much variety and change there is in the poems, and to discuss some of them more fully than before.

One way to sense the radical newness of Blake's earliest poems, is to set them side by side with what else was being written at the same time. Blake then seems to have nothing to do with convention and continuity. Here are the first eight lines of the first poem in *Poetical Sketches*:

To Spring

O thou with dewy locks, who lookest down
Thro' the clear windows of the morning, turn
Thine angel eyes upon our western isle,
Which in full choir hails thy approach, O Spring!

The hills tell each other, and the list'ning
Vallies hear; all our longing eyes are turned
Up to thy bright pavillions: issue forth,
And let thy holy feet visit our clime . . .

It happens that—if one thinks of externals not essence—there is an almost exact twin to Blake's poem. Three years later, in 1786, there appeared a volume of *Poems* by James Fordyce. This also contained an address to Spring:

Relenting Spring, who to my earnest prayer
    Hast hearken'd, and thy footsteps hither turn'd,
With those sweet smiles, and that delightful air,
    To chase the wint'ry glooms I lately mourn'd;

Hap'ly to end the elemental strife,
    And brighten universal Nature's face,
To call her various kingdoms into life,
    And lend her all thy loveliness and grace!

With thee, alluring Spring, I'll daily walk,
    Attentive listen to thy tuneful voice;
And while with thee, and God himself, I talk,
    In thy benignity and his rejoice.

Put this poem beside Blake's, and there is no need to elaborate. Fordyce says he will be "attentive" to the voice of spring, but attentive is just what he is not. Attention to the experience is set at a distance by thoughts and ideas which intrude from outside it. Fordyce does not perceive, but remember, Nature's universality and "various kingdoms". These would be available to his mind quite in spring's absence: he hurries on from spring to God. But where Blake's poem seems to open out wider than what is before his plain senses, it is not to anything available through reflection or religious generality; it is to a deeper, half-mysterious *apprehension*, playing about and over the senses, and giving them an added life.

The hills tell each other, and the list'ning
Vallies hear . . .

Something else in Blake is thrown into relief by Fordyce: Blake's awareness of the scale and subtlety and uninsistence of the coming of spring stand out against how, for the other man, everything is brusque and blunt and obvious. Fordyce makes spring sound simply like a shepherdess who walks, sings, smiles, and calls to her flocks. Then the poet walks beside her and they have a talk. In Blake's lines (I am speaking, for the moment, only of the first half of the poem, quoted above) all is hinted and remote. Spring comes only to the point where it *turns his eyes* upon the land, and the people of the land turn back their own. Nothing is blatant: they seem not actually to see the god of spring, but only his palaces somewhere in the sky. As we come to a realization of this, we sense that in this poem the god of spring is somehow one with the sun itself. It is the sun that has its "bright pavillions" in the clouds. Then, because of "dewy locks", we sense that the coming of spring is, from another standpoint, one with the coming of morning and the morning sun. And at that point, as our apprehension of the poem fills out, we realize a new exactitude in:

issue forth
And let thy holy feet visit our clime.

Blake is asking us to think, not only in the way more or less of an allegory, where it is a god that brings the spring; but also in a warmly sensuous way, so that it is also the sun that does so, as its rays come to rest on the ground, and physically move across it.

The matter is not one of simple difference between Blake and a single unknown poet, Fordyce: it is of how Blake's verse stood out generally from his time and his contemporaries. It is therefore to the point to set the latter part of 'To Spring' against another contemporary poem on the same theme. Here is part of Samuel Pratt's 'Landscapes in Verse, Taken in Spring' (1788):

> And now, again, by thy celestial power
> We taste together morning's balmy gale,
> And dash the early dew-drops from the thorn;
> We mark the maiden verdure of the spring
> Just bursting from the buds—her violets cull
> Where blue they bloom in fair humility
> Emblems of virgin grace and modest worth—
> The loveliest tenants of the lowliest hedge
> Yet sweeter than the proudest flower, that grows,
> Child of ambition, on the mountain's top.

and for comparison, the remaining eight lines of Blake's 'To Spring':

> . . . Come o'er the eastern hills, and let our winds
> Kiss thy perfumed garments; let us taste
> Thy morn and evening breath; scatter thy pearls
> Upon our love-sick land that waits for thee.
>
> O deck her forth with thy fair fingers; pour
> Thy soft kisses on her bosom; and put
> Thy golden crown upon her languish'd head
> Whose modest tresses were bound up for thee!

At a glance, it might seem as if these conventional verses by Pratt had
sensuous immediacy, while Blake's lines were more allegorical—perhaps
disquietingly so. Yet the immediacy of Pratt is a delusion. In reality he
has no interest whatsoever in the buds, the flowers, or any other such
thing. His taste is for the "emblems" of a well-worn morality. His
mountain-top flowers are invested with one moralized quality (entirely
at the expense, one cannot but add, of what any mountain flower is
really like), and his violets with another, to which their "blue" tint is
attached, at some expense of truthfulness, for the sake of assonance. The
"maiden verdure" of the spring is no better. If there is anything of
maidenliness and "virgin grace" about springtime, it is very much in a
special sense only: and it is exactly this fact that the later part of Blake's
poem, for all its personifications, brings home. We shall be naïve if we
are taken in by "love-sick" and "languish'd", and think that the poem
sees spring in the conventional terms of genteel amorousness. These are
what it has found a way of rejecting. This part of the poem has a rich if
reticent sensuousness. The lover who comes in perfumed garments,
whose breath is to be tasted, who dresses the beloved with his own hands,
who lavishes pearls on her as freely as if he were a sower and they were
the seed, who will "pour" his "soft" kisses on her bosom, and deck her
in a bridal crown, is no lover preoccupied with "virgin grace", nor one
content with any such thing. The last line clinches all. When a girl bound
up her hair, it was a sign that she knew herself for a woman; decorously,
she was stating her wish for a man. No wonder Blake made use of allegory. What he had to say about spring, was forceful enough to gain
force from being expressed with reticence. His poem is an intimation of
spring's universal life-giving procreation; and it is this which obliges one
in the end to dismiss Pratt's line as (if we are to speak plainly) contemp-
tible nonsense.

One more poem on spring from the 1780's: it is by Mrs. Barbauld, a member of the circle that visited at the Rev. Henry Mathew's house. Blake must have known her, and it is beyond question that her work influenced his own (we shall come back to this in Chapter 2). Today she is under-rated as a poet: that is to say, she is wholly forgotten, which is to go just a little far. Her 'Ode to Spring' with its ". . . silent dews that swell/*The milky ear's green stem*" can still please by its occasional freshness, and its intricate movement:

> Sweet daughter of a rough and stormy sire,
> Hoar Winter's blooming child; delightful Spring!
>   Whose unshorn locks with leaves
>   And swelling buds are crown'd;
>
> From the green islands of eternal youth,
> (Crown'd with fresh blooms, and ever springing shade,)
>   Turn, hither turn thy step,
>   O thou, whose powerful voice
>
> More sweet than softest touch of Doric reed,
> Or Lydian flute, can sooth the madding winds,
>   And thro' the stormy deep
>   Breathe thy own tender calm.
>
> Thee, best belov'd! the virgin train await
> With songs and festal rites, and joy to rove
>   Thy blooming wilds among,
>   And vales and dewy lawns,
>
> With untir'd feet; and cull thy earliest sweets
> To weave fresh garlands for the glowing brow
>   Of him, the favour'd youth
>   That prompts their whisper'd sigh.
>
> Unlock thy copious stores; those tender showers
> That drop their sweetness on the infant buds,
>   And silent dews that swell
>   The milky ear's green stem.
>
> And feed the flowering osier's early shoots;
> And call those winds which thro' the whispering boughs
>   With warm and pleasant breath
>   Salute the blowing flowers.
>
> Now let me sit beneath the whitening thorn,
> And mark thy spreading tints steal o'er the dale;
>   And watch with patient eye
>   Thy fair unfolding charms . . .

Mrs. Barbauld is not another Fordyce or Pratt. One cannot read those lines without interest. Yet there is no need to go further than to take note of their weakest point, in order to recognize how Blake's poem achieves something of quite a different order. That weakest point lies surely in the line, "From the green islands of eternal youth". But it is not enough merely to dislike this as a sudden lapse into abstraction. The change has a substantial cause. It is that (apart perhaps from the end of the next stanza) this is the only point in the whole poem—not merely the lines quoted— where the author strives to make her picture of Spring something other than a straightforward, even a realistic, pastoral scene. If there is allegory, it is a novelistic or perhaps one should say novelettish allegory. In Blake's poem some kind of visionary apprehension made the people of the allegory quite unlike those of a natural landscape; and the same is true of the other poems in the set of four, on the four seasons, which opens *Poetical Sketches*. There is Summer, passing through the valleys on his fierce steeds, pitching his "golden tent" and, when noon "rode o'er the deep of heaven" in his chariot, throwing off his draperies and rushing into the stream; or Autumn "stained/With the blood of the grape", who rested for a while and sang, but then

> . . . rose, girded himself and o'er the bleak
> Hills fled from our sight; but left his golden load.

—and there is Winter, who "rides heavy" over the deep sea, and "takes his seat upon the cliffs". Each time, Blake's vision of the spirit of the season is far from anything conventionally pastoral, or indeed from anything realistic at all. It is intense and idiosyncratic, it seems to work in an unfamiliar dimension and create something like a new world. Mrs. Barbauld's figure of Spring is a charming girl, Blake's is protagonist in something like a new myth.

In fact, Mrs. Barbauld's poem has a strikingly obvious poetic antecedent in the time just before it. Its Horatian stanza-pattern, its intricacy, and many of its details (the "virgin train", the "flowering osier", the "softest influence" and the catalogue of other seasons which comes at the end of the poem, not quoted above), all help one to see how much it owes to a much more accomplished piece in the same vein: Collins' *Ode to Evening*. One must admit, if it comes to this, that Blake's early poems also suggest that he knew this particular poem; as, from time to time, they show mannerisms or movements of thought characteristic of a good deal of eighteenth-century verse (" . . . more than mortal fire/Burns in my soul, and does my song inspire"; "And the vale darkens at my pen-sive woe"). But even in *Poetical Sketches*, where Blake is at the very beginning of his career, what links him with Collins or Gray or Akenside is trivial as against what sets him in contrast to them.

'To the Muses', another poem in *Poetical Sketches*, makes the point well:

> Whether on Ida's shady brow,
> Or in the chambers of the East,
> The chambers of the sun, that now
> From ancient melody have ceas'd;
>
> Whether in Heaven ye wander fair,
> Or the green corners of the earth,
> Or the blue regions of the air
> Where the melodious winds have birth;
>
> Whether on crystal rocks ye rove,
> Beneath the bosom of the sea
> Wand'ring in many a coral grove,
> Fair Nine, forsaking Poetry!
>
> How have you left the ancient love
> That bards of old enjoy'd in you!
> The languid strings do scarcely move!
> The sound is forc'd, the notes are few.

Blake uses the familiar classical conception of the "Fair Nine", just as Gray does in his Pindaric ode 'The Progress of Poesy'. But while Gray closes his poem with a modestly complacent review of the situation in verse in his own time and place, the very point of Blake's is that his own time is one of poetic dearth. The "sound is forc'd": there is something, this must mean, factitious and ungenuine in what is being written. Again, Gray opens his poem with the general idea of Greek classical poetry ("Helicon's harmonious springs"); Blake looks elsewhere. He has no interest in what Gray calls the "warbled lay" of Greek verse. 'To the Muses' sees the true creator of poetry as less the Muse than the Bard. Mount "Ida's shady brow" must point to Homer; and as for Blake's other starting-point, the "chambers of the East" that once produced poetry but now do so no more, can refer only to the prophetic Hebrew bards of the Old Testament. The phrase "chambers of the sun" puts this beyond doubt as soon as we see where Blake has taken it from: ". . . the sun, which is as a bridegroom coming out of his chamber" (*Psalm* xix, 5).

At this stage of the discussion I do not want to raise in full the question of how much Blake owed his lyric or other poetry to the Bible. That is a large issue, and will turn out to be in no sense one of verbal borrowings, but of a whole mode of vision and a whole world of the imagination. In the next chapter, moreover, I hope to show that this side of his work is no matter of the Bible alone, but of the Bible, and the World of the Bible, as Blake knew these both directly, and through the writings of others who had drawn on it before him. But for the present, the point is really that Blake's 'To Spring' has that extra and visionary dimension very largely because it sees its subject in Biblical terms. It has such a sense of its subject as Blake could find in scripture, while Mrs. Barbauld's sense of hers was what she could find in Collins (as Collins, in part, had found his in Horace).

One reason why Blake stood in such a contrast to most of his contemporaries was undoubtedly that he looked back to this other, this altogether more solemn and profound, source of inspiration. If we try to open the subject on a limited scale for the present, one way of seeing how much the Bible meant to Blake is to notice the last item in *Poetical Sketches*: a substantial prose narrative entitled 'Samson', freely retold from the *Book of Judges*, adhering closely to the language of the biblical narrative at many points, and linking in expression also with the *Book of Isaiah*. If we look again at 'To Spring' in the light of this, what transpires is that the Biblical echoes are no merely verbal matter, but what largely help to create Blake's personal mode of vision in the poem. The "clear windows of the morning" echo *Malachi*, III, 10:

> I will . . . open you the windows of heaven, and pour you out a blessing.

The lines about the hills and valleys recall passages from the *Psalms*:

> thou crownest the year with thy goodness . . . the little hills rejoice on every side . . . the valleys . . . shout for joy, they also sing (LXV, 11–13: cf. also CXIV, 4).

The "dewy locks" of Spring, the phrase perhaps above all others which invests the allegory with the sensuous quality of a real spring-morning landscape, is an idea from the *Song of Songs*:

> my head is filled with dew, and my locks with the drops of the night (V, 2).

Finally, the third and fourth stanzas, where the rich lover crowns his humble beloved (Blake uses the word "modest") present a situation like that of the *Song of Songs* as a whole.

There is no great interest in the fact that Blake's poetry seems to have been influenced by his knowledge of scripture, unless one goes on, by the help of this knowledge, to identify some quality in his work which as a result is there first-hand. This connexion has already been made above to some extent, but a full discussion of it must wait till the next chapter. By the same token, when we are told (as we often are, and justly) that Blake's lyrics owe a good deal to Shakespeare, the stress must fall on just what aspect of Shakespeare's verse most kindled his mind and enriched his work.

It would be easy to make a mistake about this. Blake's most obvious "imitations" of Shakespeare are the long dramatic fragment *King Edward the Third*, and the *Prologue*. 'Intended for a Dramatic Piece of King Edward the Fourth'. Both of these are in *Poetical Sketches*, and both show Blake imitating the rhetorical style that he found in Shakespeare's history plays.

> O for a voice like thunder, and a tongue
> To drown the throat of war!

the *Prologue* begins; one recalls the Prologue to *Henry V*:

> O for a Muse of fire, that would ascend
> The brightest heaven of invention . . . !

King Edward the Third shows much of the same:

> . . . 'tis with princes as 'tis with the sun,
> If not sometimes o'er-clouded, we grow weary
> Of his officious glory

—those lines will make readers think of Prince Hal's famous soliloquy in I *Henry IV*. But had Shakespeare written only in the high style like this, even he would have been a bore; and closer reading makes it plain that Blake did not simply draw rhetoric from him—nor even chiefly so. Passages from Blake's fragment, like the two which follow, recall Vernon's description of Hal before the battle of Shrewsbury; but it is not that note they culminate in. Blake has found something else in Shakespeare also, and it is something that meant incomparably more to his own experience and cast of mind:

> He is a young lion. O I have seen him fight,
> And give command, and lightning has flashed
> From his eyes across the field; I have seen him
> Shake hands with death, and strike a bargain for
> The enemy; *he has danced in the field*
> *Of truth, like a youth at morrice play.* (iii, 26–31)

> Now my heart dances, and I am as light
> As the young bridegroom going to be married.
> Now must I to my soldiers, get them ready,
> Furbish our armours bright, new plume our helms,
> And we will sing, *like the young housewives busied*
> *In the dairy.* (iii, 144–9)

Central to Shakespeare, as everyone knows, is his profoundly humane sense of how the great and public affairs of life are one with its simplest and lowliest ones, and cannot but be seen alongside them. It is this that Blake recreates in the passages I have just quoted. Then, when one turns from that early and experimental piece, to Blake's real achievement, in the lyrics, it is clearer still that here is what he most has in common with Shakespeare. I have touched on how there is something solemn and visionary in Blake; but what really distinguishes his verse is a power to make this one with a rustic, pastoral world—not a literary and conventionalized pastoralism, but the real life of the country.

> When the voices of children are heard on the green
> ('Nurses song')

> The distant huntsman sounds his horn,
> And the sky-lark sings with me
> ('The School Boy')

Most mid-eighteenth-century poets entered this realm with more or less of difficulty. Their stance as poets was literary and formal. Their work gives the impression of looking at the countryside down from above. If any earlier writer helped Blake to do otherwise, it was Shakespeare; and this was so because Shakespeare was himself, from one standpoint, a folk author, a great representative of the common mind.

Blake's link with this side of Shakespeare is already clear in *Poetical Sketches*. The 'Song' which begins:

> Memory, hither come,
> And tune your merry notes

is clearly based on Shakespeare's 'Under the Greenwood Tree' in *As You Like It*. 'Mad Song' has the lines:

> But lo! the morning peeps
> Over the eastern steeps,
> And the *rustling* birds of dawn
> The earth do scorn.

Here, a sound-echo that has no relation to the sense helps to make it seem likely that Blake is recalling how Shakespeare, in *Hamlet*, likens the morning to a figure in the countryman's dress of the time:

> But look, the morn, in *russet* mantle clad,
> Walks o'er the dew of yon high eastward hill.

Again, Blake's poem 'Blind Man's Buff' is largely a pastiche of Puck's account of country pastimes in *A Midsummer Night's Dream*; and 'Song by an Old Shepherd' (one of three lyrics that were written out in a copy of *Poetical Sketches*, and probably composed about four years after those poems were published) combines clear echoes from Shakespeare's "When icicles hang by the wall" (*Love's Labour's Lost*), and "Blow, blow, thou winter wind" (*As You Like It*).

So this is no matter of any general "influence" of Shakespeare on Blake; but of one particular point at which the later writer found something especially meaningful to him in the earlier one. What Blake seized on was Shakespeare the recorder of common life: the writer, one might say, of songs of the people. By the same token, if one uses the word "pastoral" of something in Blake, it is for a pastoralism in firm contrast to the pastoralism of Pope, and much nearer to that of "And Dick the shepherd blows his nail". In fact, it is something that in part is based on that very phrase.

Shakespeare's "Blow, blow, thou winter wind" is especially to the point. This lyric, with its:

> Freeze, Freeze, thou bitter sky
> Thou dost not bite so nigh
> As benefits forgot

—and the rest, is in fact almost a string of country proverbs. The proverb is an aspect of the common mind that seems to have fascinated Blake. So far as I know, he is the only major English writer himself to have composed a whole collection of proverbs. "The sayings used in a nation", he wrote, "mark its character." The proverbs in *The Marriage of Heaven and*

Hell come early in Blake's work. But 'Auguries of Innocence' (*c.* 1803) is, throughout, something not far short of a string of proverbs in verse form:

> He who shall hurt the little Wren
> Shall never be belov'd by Men . . .
> The poor man's Farthing is worth more
> Than all the Gold on Afric's Shore . . .
> If the Sun and Moon should doubt
> They'd immediately Go out.

Quite possibly, in fact, the first of all the couplets in this poem is not a composed but a genuine folk-saying:

> A robin in a cage
> Sets all heaven in a rage.

is recorded as an ordinary English proverb in *All the Year Round* (July 14th, 1888), without any mention of Blake.[1]

To sum up. Wherever one turns in Blake's lyrics, the impress of popular verse tradition is inescapably clear. It shows in the most unexpected places. I shall have much to say about the metres of the lyrics in the next chapter: here it is perhaps not out of place to remark, in passing, how the metre of Blake's most vehement, impassioned lyric is the same as that of a light-hearted nursery rhyme. It is difficult to think this is an accident, moreover, when the actual visual Gestalt is so much the same:

> Tyger, tyger, burning bright
> In the forests of the night . . .

> Twinkle, twinkle, little star . . .
> Like a diamond in the sky.

Perhaps there is here even some conscious reversal, on Blake's part, of the mood of the earlier piece. If so, it is not (as will transpire) by any means the only case of that.

The clearest instance of how Blake drew on the traditions of our popular literature relates to 'My Pretty Rose Tree' in *Songs of Experience*. As with 'Tyger, tyger' the connexion is one of thought, not words alone; but in this case it so much creates Blake's poem as a whole, that that had better be quoted in full:

[1] Reprinted in G. F. Northall, *English Folk-Rhymes* (1892), p. 276.

A flower was offer'd to me,
Such a flower as May never bore;
But I said 'I've a Pretty Rose-tree,'
And I passed the sweet flower o'er.

Then I went to my Pretty Rose-tree,
To tend her by day and by night;
But my Rose turn'd away with jealousy,
And her thorns were my only delight.

Blake has reversed the sexes, but in that poem the movement of thought,
the imagery, and (one might add) the metre, are close indeed to one of
our most beautiful folk-songs:

I sowed the seeds of love,
'Twas early in the spring,
In April and May, and in June likewise,
The small birds they do sing . . .

My gardener he stood by,
I asked him to choose for me,
He chose me the violet, the lily and the pink,
But these I refused all three.

The violet I forsook
Because it fades so soon.
The lily and the pink I did overlook
And I vowed I'd stay till June.

For in June there's a red rosebud,
And that's the flower for me,
So I pulled and plucked at the red rosebud,
Till I gained the willow tree . . .

My gardener he stood by,
And he told me to take good care;
For in the middle of the red rosebud
There grew a sharp thorn there.

I told him I'd take no care
Until I felt the smart.
I pulled and I plucked at the red rosebud
Till it pierced me to the heart.[1]

Again, one ought perhaps to insist that there is no question of imitation

[1] Text from *The Idiom of the People*, ed. J. Reeves; 1961 edn., p. 194.

or borrowing merely at the verbal level. Among his other gifts, Blake had access to the popular mode of vision and expression *as wholes*.

That this was no isolated personal phenomenon in his time is perfectly true; if the general literary history of the later eighteenth century were at issue, rather than Blake's lyrics in particular, then Cowper's 'John Gilpin', Wordsworth's *Lyrical Ballads*, and 'The Ancient Mariner' would all form part of the story. But in none of these did the impulse towards popular poetry operate at so profound a level, or modify the writer's apprehension of life as much as it did in Blake. Wordsworth (or at least, his *persona* in the poem) talks to Alice Fell after "alighting on the ground" from the post-chaise. Here, he certainly sees rural life down from above. Alice calls him "sir", he calls her "child", and makes the landlord, his agent, buy her a new cloak. Blake belonged to the people and could catch the exact note of popular verse, could enter into its very soul. Perhaps the clearest way of all to see this, is to read the following Gloucestershire folk lullaby, recorded from about 1840.[1] I do not think it could possibly have been an actual *product* of Blake's lyric; but even should this be so, the essential point remains, because it is one that relates not to literary influence, but immediate poetic quality. That there may also be a hint or so of the Victorian ballad, slightly confusing the older, folk quality, is also beside the point:

> Sleep, baby, sleep,
> Our cottage vale is deep;
> The little lamb is on the green
> With woolly fleece so soft and clean
> Sleep, baby, sleep!
>
> Sleep, baby, sleep,
> Down where the woodbines creep;
> Be always like the lamb so mild,
> A kind, and sweet, and gentle child—
> Sleep, baby, sleep.[1]

Some of the points made so far ought now to be resumed. If, in reading Blake, we keep in mind the strength and prominence of the Bible as an influence, and also of the traditions of popular literature, we shall in quite large part know what to look for, and what not to look for. If we

[1] Northall, *op. cit.*, p. 428-9.

are going to find subtleties in Blake's lyrics, they ought, probably, to be subtleties which are somehow in accordance with these modes of composition; they may augment or enrich, but ought in all probability not to be such as leave no place for them. There may, indeed, be wealth of meaning, but we shall be wise to look for it as we would look for wealth of meaning in an Old Testament symbolic passage, or a New Testament parable, or even a proverb.

There is a short poem in *Songs of Experience* called 'The Lilly', which most critics virtually ignore, but which makes the point well:

> The modest Rose puts forth a thorn,
> The humble Sheep a threat'ning horn;
> While the Lilly white shall in Love delight,
> Nor a thorn, nor a threat, stain her beauty bright.

The poem begins with what is in effect a traditional proverb ("no rose without a thorn") and the whole of it makes up what has something of the appearance of a proverbial maxim in the form of a simple quatrain. Where ought reading such a poem to start? From a consideration, let us say, of that passage in the *Song of Songs* which had long established the lily and the rose as somehow *fundamental* emblems of the love-situation:

> I am the rose of Sharon, and the lily of the valleys.
> As the lily among thorns, so is my love among the daughters.
> (*Cant.* 2, 1)

Blake's poem, it would now seem, gains its point, its pointedness, from the radical contrast around which it is arranged. Gentle things divide into those like the rose whose gentleness is marred by something incompatible with gentleness, and those like the lily (traditional symbol—as in 'The Seeds of Love'—of purity) in which there is no false note, in which all is brightness and beauty.

Only one difficulty besets this reading: that the poem is among the *Songs of Experience*, and such a celebration of unmarred purity and harmlessness ought not to be a Song of Experience at all, but a Song of Innocence. Once call this to mind, though, and the radical contrast (rose/lily) around which it seemed that the poem had been built, in no way disappears. It begins, rather, to transpire as the very opposite of what it first seemed. The lily, it now transpires, must be one of the flowers that grow in 'The Garden of Love' (the next poem in the collection) after the "priests in black gowns" have taken it over, and set "Thou shalt not"

above their chapel door. If it delights in love, that must be sanctimoniously
and self-absorbedly all talk and no do. And at this point certain verbal
subtleties in the quatrain indeed become relevant and fall into place: we
recall, for example, the traditional notion that the abandonment of
virginity goes with a "stain" on whiteness which could be likened to the
"modest" (the blushing) rose. What this lily delights in is not love but
"love": the cant term that would have been dear to the love-mouthing
but murderous priest in another poem in the collection: 'A Little Boy
Lost'. The draft of the poem in the 1793 *Notebook* includes two lines later
omitted:

> ... While the lilly white shall in love delight,
>> *And the lion increase freedom and peace*
>> *The priest loves war and the soldier peace*

In so far as we may allow these to guide us towards an understanding of
the poem in its final form, they seem to put it beyond doubt, that the
lily is a sham. The point of this discussion, though, is not simply to
interpret this one poem, but to see that what gave it its point was a kind
of radical simplicity of emblem-structure: though what gave it its full
point, was that that structure proved in the end to be the very opposite
of what it seemed at first.

'The Lilly' is far from being among Blake's most important lyrics
(though far more forceful and meaningful than is usually seen); and the
most important thing to take away from this discussion of the poem is,
in all probability, a clearer sense of the *mode* of writing which Blake so
often employs. It is a mode which is very common in the Bible, and also
in our popular literature (the proverb, the folk-rhyme); and this is why
it is helpful to recognize how near to those Blake is in his work and how
much he owes to them. The mode that I have in mind is what we
encounter when a poet is asking us to contemplate something not, as he
realizes it for us (richly and idiosyncratically) by his texture of language;
but in its simplicity, in its starkness. Then the language of the poem does
its work by being somehow *transparent*; and the subject gains pregnancy
of meaning—at least to begin with—because of how it stands in a revela-
tory position (maybe a central, maybe an extreme one) seen across the
whole spectrum of our existence.

A number of Blake's lyrics are of this kind: we complicate them at our
peril, at least unless we start from the position of their radical simplicity
first. 'The Sick Rose', for example, is a memorable poem in the first

place because it presents us with the feud between the most conspicuous, opulent and beautiful thing we know, and what is most secret, pallid (the "worm" in the poem is in one aspect a maggot) and repulsive. Job at his most moving can rely on the same unadorned presentation of extremes:

> they change the night into day . . . the grave is mine house . . .
> I have said to the worm, thou art my mother (XVII, 13–14)

Consider other poems. In 'The Fly', experience is seen as it were between its two extreme poles, man the lord of creation (not, of course, an idea from Darwinism, but from *Genesis* I, 26) and the weakest and frailest of created things. 'Infant Joy' is a dialogue between two extremes of human life; the helpless new-born child, and the all-protective mother who (I, 11) sings to it. 'The Shepherd' presents the all-protective guardian, and the gentlest of animals (again, this is a poem of which more must be said later). 'The Lamb' sets animal and childish innocence side by side. 'The Chimney Sweeper' (in *Songs of Innocence*) brings together the gentleness of childhood, with its innate power for joy, and perhaps the foulest thing that, in Blake's time, it might be forced into.

'The Blossom' is a more difficult case. Several critics have interpreted it as a complicated and even profound poem. Wicksteed[1] saw it as symbolic of love and sexual intercourse, and D. J. Gillham, in one of the most recent studies of Blake's lyrics,[2] so much takes this idea for granted that he merely adverts to it in a parenthesis. "Sexual intimacy", he goes on, is a subject particularly well suited to Blake's purpose in establishing a gulf between Innocence and Experience. This belief Mr. Gillham apparently elicits not from something out of Blake's verse, but from his own findings in matters sexual: sexual intimacy is "either very wonderful or most distressing". When he reverts to the poem, he is none too happy with it. "The blossom herself, despite her tenderness, . . . tends to be aware of the male sexual organ almost as a sort of pet."

Readers must decide, without guidance from me, how far Mr. Gillham's efforts as a sexual informant will satisfy or interest them. But that last remark is silly enough to discredit this whole way of reading the poem. Writing about sexual intercourse in terms of a robin, a sparrow and a flower is in any case hardly like Blake. Three or four years later, he was to express himself very much otherwise:

[1] Joseph H. Wicksteed, *Blake's Innocence and Experience* (1928), pp. 125–8.
[2] *Blake's Contrary States* (1966), pp. 164–5.

> In a wife I would desire
> What in whores is always found—
> The lineaments of Gratified desire.

But besides this, the whole enterprise of interpretation along these lines is open to a decisive objection: it turns a good poem into a bad one. We start with a brief poem, but one full of life; a poem gay yet poignant, simple-seeming yet suggestive of a hidden fulness, plain yet vivid. Even at first reading, and while we still sense that we have not fully grasped its meaning, it gives us abundant and immediate interest and pleasure. We end with something in a kind of heavy-handed cipher; and not only does it strike us, once we have deciphered it, as a ridiculous and unnecessary way of wrapping up something about "sexual intimacy"; it is so particularly ridiculous as to be aware of the male sexual organ as a sort of pet. There is really nothing to say but that all this is quite out of the question. If this is Blake, he warrants jettisoning.

E. D. Hirsch, rightly stressing the fact that, in all his printings of *Songs of Innocence*, Blake puts 'The Blossom' immediately next to 'The Lamb', argues that this makes it unlikely for the poem to be devoted to sexuality.[1] But instead, he gives it another elaborate meaning: in fact, he tries out several. The speaker is Earth, and the poem explores the distinction between the "insentient and unconscious" life of plants, by comparison with the "more human dimension" represented by the birds; or alternatively, the blossom symbolizes birth, and the two birds respectively symbolize the soul on its way towards birth, and the soul imprisoned, after birth, in the body. The objection to these interpretations is much like that to what Mr. Gillham put forward: they turn a good poem into a bad. On these terms, the poem would *reveal* nothing to us about different levels of life, or about the soul before and after birth. Everything which we found in it about these matters, we should have to bring to it. In itself, it would be nothing but a sort of minimal, arbitrary, and so wholly tedious *encoding* of them. If we think it is this, we deprive it of merit.

'The Blossom' is admittedly a difficult poem, though apparently so artless. But again, I wish to suggest that we come nearest to solving the difficulties if we give it meaning on the simplest terms we can find. On this basis, it seems doubtful that the speaker will be Earth, because that

[1] *Innocence and Experience: An Introduction to Blake* (1964), pp. 181–4. Even when one disagrees with it, this book is informed, penetrating and rewarding.

would make the poem so surprisingly, so obscurely different from the others in the collection ('Earth's Answer' in *Songs of Experience*, is a different and special case, and Blake also gave it a clear label). Over and over, in *Songs of Innocence*, if the speaker of the poem is not the poet himself, it is a child. For 'The Blossom' to be spoken by a young girl (as its constant companion, 'The Lamb' is apparently spoken by a boy) is therefore the simplest hypothesis. Only if it is one impossible to sustain ought the reader to abandon it and try something more elaborate. "Quite remarkably," writes Hirsch, "everything seems to happen near the speaker's bosom." Remarkable, perhaps, but not difficult on that account, if one thinks of how girls pluck flowers in spring-time, and where, often enough, they put them when they have plucked them. The flower, it then transpires, sees things near the girl's bosom simply because it sees them near where it is. Then (since the robin's "sobbing" need not in Blake's time have meant sorrow), we have a poem which celebrates the beauty and gaiety of the season of blossom and growth. Green leaves, twittering or singing birds, blooming flower and girl with her young bosom (it is not essential to think of her as mature, only old enough to know where her bosom is and what it is going to be for) belong simply but jubilantly together. The poem calls on the simplest realities of even a child's experience. Once again, we come nearest to understanding it *as a success* when we avoid sophisticating it.

'The Little Boy Lost' and 'The Little Boy Found' (in *Songs of Innocence*) have also caused critics like Hirsch and Erdmann difficulty.[1] "Away the vapour flew", they suppose must mean that it deserted the lost child, and so had a conscious will and therefore a symbolic meaning. Erdman takes it for the concept of an "impersonal God" to contrast with the father-like figure of the companion poem: the pair then become a brief guide to deism and theism.

But one should remember, rather, the real danger there once was of being led astray in darkness by marsh-lights, and the real dangers of children getting lost in rural England. Wordsworth's *Idiot Boy* depends on the meaningfulness of the same idea. Once this simple fact of rural life in an earlier time is called to mind, the two poems belong to *Songs of Innocence*, as a pair, because together they show the indifference of the world to the needs of the innocent (". . . away the vapour flew") as illusory: a benevolent world ("God, ever nigh") takes care of little

[1] Hirsch, *op. cit.*, pp. 186–8; David V. Erdman, *Blake: Prophet Against Empire* (1954), p. 115.

children and of distraught parents too. If we are too sophisticated to feel this simple need, we shall fail over the simple suggestion of joyful reassurance.

But the interest of these lyrics, their power to fill the memory and hold the imagination, is no result merely of how in writing them Blake often chose subjects of a radical, even an archetypal simplicity. Unobtrusively but decisively, most of the poems are memorable through their form. If the two stanzas in 'The Blossom' are transposed, the poem is spoilt: the true climax of this short song to spring is that the life of spring is itself song. Brief as they are, Blake's lyrics conceal—or conceal from the careless reader—a range and rigour of development which sometimes invites even the word spectacular. 'To Spring', we saw, began with a somehow remote, other-worldly contrast between the earth and what seems like the god of the season; yet in the course of the poem, this remote relation is transformed into that between two lovers preparing together for a marriage, or indeed for its consummation. At the end of sixteen lines, we find ourselves, almost without realizing how, in a new world. The first poem in *Songs of Innocence* is another example. About the full unity of this more must be said later; but for the present, one need only notice its continuous momentum of development. First, the piper pipes his melodies in seeming light-hearted idleness and gaiety. Then, at the call of the child, he selects one on a particular theme. Next he moves a step further away from casual spontaneity, and plays the chosen piece a second time. Next, melody alone is not enough: the tune ("the same", notice) is repeated once more, but, sung with its words. Finally comes the process of making pen and ink and recording the songs permanently, and not for one child but for all:

> Piping down the valleys wild,
> Piping songs of pleasant glee,
> On a cloud I saw a child,
> And he laughing said to me:
>
> 'Pipe a song about a Lamb!'
> So I piped with merry cheer.
> 'Piper, pipe that song again;'
> So I piped: he wept to hear.
>
> 'Drop thy pipe, thy happy pipe;
> Sing thy songs of happy cheer:'
> So I sang the same again,
> While he wept with joy to hear.

'Piper, sit thee down and write
In a book, that all may read.'
So he vanish'd from my sight,
And I pluck'd a hollow reed,

And I made a rural pen,
And I stain'd the water clear,
And I wrote my happy songs
Every child may joy to hear.

Seemingly, one of the simplest poems among all the *Songs of Innocence* is 'Infant Joy'. The reader might see the poem as almost without content: a poem of innocent yet empty lispings such as might come from an infant child. Yet, once again, a closer look shows point and pointedness and development. By the end of the first stanza, something has been suggested about the world, as well as about simply the child and the mother.

'Joy is my name'
Sweet joy befall thee.

The world is a place at least potentially of joy, it has power to warrant such a name for a child. But "Joy is my name" does not mean exactly the same as the line preceding it. "I happy am"); or rather, can mean more than that. Whose joy, after all, is most obvious in the poem itself?—

Sweet joy I call thee

says the mother in the middle of the next stanza, in the first line that is really more than repetition.

Thou dost smile,
I sing the while . . .

The mother has her joy also, and the "Sweet joy befall thee" refrain comes with a new dimension of meaning in the second stanza: disregard the quotation marks, and the child could as well be saying this to the mother as the mother to her; or the poet himself be saying it to her. Moreover, her joy is a confirmation of how her call for joy to "befall" her baby daughter will not, in all likelihood, be empty. The poem brings us, at its close, to the point of seeing that the world is a place where humans are born into joy by the very fact that humans are born at all. Birth is simply one and the same with the great joy of motherhood. The generations are made one by a joint heritage of fruitfulness and innocence.

'London', in *Songs of Experience*, is in many ways at the other extreme from 'Infant Joy'; but it too is a poem which gains integration and power from development. The ringing repetitions of stanza I, "mark . . . mark . . . mark . . ." (Blake achieved this effect only through successive drafts, and one is reminded of the recurrent "mark this . . . mark this" of his *Marginalia*) stress the admonitory solemnity of the poem. But admonition which does not gather strength as it proceeds must lose it instead, and become no more than wearisome. Blake's poem gathers strength because as it proceeds it plunges so much deeper into the horrors of the anti-'innocence' world: moves, in short, from the "charter'd street" of stanza I, to the "midnight streets" of stanza IX.

Where are these horrors? First, in relatively innocuous form, as mere "marks of weakness", and quite generally. But immediately there is a change from marks of weakness to "marks of woe"; and in the second stanza, from mere "mark" of grief to the "cry" which seems to come from every man and every child too—in fact the stanza suggests a world of universal lamentation and cursing. When generality is narrowed (in stanza III) to particularity, it is at first a particularity, whether childlike in the sweep or adult in the soldier, that the general reader may feel does not touch him. But in the fourth stanza, particularity itself gathers power and comes nearer home: one may safeguard oneself and one's children from the fates of child sweep or soldier, but to do so from the youthful harlot and her "plagues" is not quite so certain. Nor is this the real point. In the closing lines:

> the youthful harlot's curse
> Blasts the new-born Infant's tear

Doubtless the literal sense is that the child whore is cursing her own child; but what the poem demands to know is whether *any* child can be unblighted where, one and all, the new-born may come to youthful harlotry or, I suppose, to being its clients. By now Blake's poem has reached a point where it shows that the birthright of one and all is a world blighted through and through. His poem by now shows up the falsity of the central and most sacred institutions of every "charter'd street" of respectability. Not physical infection, but the accursed nature of the whole anti-innocence world, is what shows up the innermost shrine of polite society as a universe-of-death transformation of itself: as, in short—

> . . . the Marriage *hearse*

There is the explosive phrase which concludes this masterpiece of developing form. It gives to 'London' the most powerful closing line of any poem known to me in any language.

2. Tradition and Logic

There are indeed continuities of one kind and another between *Poetical Sketches* and Blake's later lyrics, but there is a great contrast too. *Poetical Sketches* is an experimental work, with more or less unrelated poems in many varied styles; but *Songs of Innocence* and *Songs of Experience* are unified. To read the poems in these two collections as no more than isolated lyrics is half to throw them away.

It is at this point that one must take stock of how firmly Blake's poems belong to traditions of composition that run back through the eighteenth century and indeed before it; and must expand the picture which was no more than begun as a sketch, when Blake's contact with Shakespeare and popular literature was emphasized, or even his contact with the Bible. To begin with, the continuity to which Blake's work belongs is simply not what it has sometimes been taken to be. What has to be seen behind his work is something far richer and more distinctive than the eighteenth-century ballad as represented, for example, by Thomas Durfey's 'Pills to Purge Melancholy' (1719–20).[1] It is true that Blake may have known these poems, but the notion that they could stand as models for his lyrics cannot survive reading beyond their first lines. It is all very well to sense something like Blake in:

> The bonny grey Ey'd Morn began to peep . . .

Maybe there is something here a little like the lyrics for morning in *Poetical Sketches*—the 'Song', for example, which begins:

> When early morn walks forth in sober grey;
> Then to my black ey'd maid I haste away . . .

or the lines in another 'Song' which run:

> My feet are wing'd, while o'er the dewy lawn
> I meet my maiden, risen like the morn . . .

But Durfey's text continues:

> . . . When Jockey rowz'd with love came blithely on. (III, 234)

[1] See F. W. Bateson, *Selected Poems of William Blake* (1957), p. xvii.

Another of Durfey's collection opens:

> The Lark awakes the drowzy morn

but as its second line it has:

> My dearest lovely *Chloe* rise.

Another, again perhaps suggesting something of Blake, opens:

> Maiden fresh as a rose . . .

It goes on:

> Young, buxom and full of jollity
> Take no Spouse among Beaux,
> Fond of their raking quality . . .

If we stress the "popular" quality in Blake's lyrics, it must be a popular something that is in another world from Tony Lumpkin.

Writers on Blake like Mona Wilson, Vivian de Sola Pinto, and A. P. Davis have noticed the connexion between Blake and Isaac Watts,[1] but none of them have brought out just how much Blake belongs to a tradition of hymn-writing that runs steadily throughout the century; and moreover how he does not just belong to this tradition, but also challenges it in a radical way.

Take a simple point first: it is the hymn which provides a perspective for one of the most immediately striking things in the lyrics, their varied use of metres, and the way in which, to a reader coming from the "literary" verse of the eighteenth century, these metres seem highly original. But at the same time, this originality is entirely different from that, say, of Herbert. Blake's 'Songs' are *songs*. Every lyric (save 'The Voice of the Ancient Bard', appended to *Songs of Innocence* long after the collection was completed) is stanzaic, as if it were truly to be set to a repeated melody. There is only one poem, 'The Little Black Boy', in ten-syllable lines, and none of the metres lends itself less to a lyrical than to a thoughtful or discursive tone. Cases where the sense is not complete, or substantially so, by the line-end, are extraordinarily rare. What we have is remarkable variety of a kind that goes with great simplicity and in a sense transparency of both structure and meaning. The contrast with earlier "literary" lyric poets is very clear.

[1] Mona Wilson, *The Life of William Blake*: 1948 edn., p. 28. V. de Sola Pinto, 'Isaac Watts and William Blake': *Review of English Studies*, 1944, p. 214. A. P. Davis, *Isaac Watts, his Life and Work* (N.Y., 1943), pp. 228 ff.

Blake in one respect departed from what was at least most usual in contemporary hymn-writing, and followed a practice common enough in the lyric throughout the whole of the eighteenth century, in that he made frequent use of triple rhythms. But for the most part he did this so that the triple rhythms combined freely with rhythms that were iambic or trochaic:

> How can a bird that is born for joy
> Sit in a cage and sing? ('The School Boy')

> Lark in Sky
> Merrily
> Merrily, merrily, to welcome in the Year. ('Spring')

He very often has trochaic rhythms in short lyrics, and this is very like the hymns of his time (or indeed of later time). Blake drew a great deal on his own invention, in using or combining such varied metres, and in creating such a variety of stanza patterns. But the metrical and stanzaic variety of the hymns themselves was much greater than in lyric poetry in Blake's time. This came about because there were many varied, traditional, and well-loved melodies, and these gave their own shape to words written for them: hymn-writing was largely not the setting of words to music, but the writing of words for it.

Perhaps one clear way to show how much hymn metric has to do with Blake is to review the *Songs of Innocence* poems in order.

'Introduction' ("Piping down the valleys wild,/Piping songs of pleasant glee"), and 'A Dream' ("Once a dream did weave a shade/O'er my Angel-guarded bed"), are both in the four-line seven-syllable trochaic measure of, for example, Charles Wesley's:

> Christ the Lord is ris'n today,
> Sons of men and angels, say . . .

'The Little Girl Lost' (beginning "In futurity/I prophetic see . . ."), and its companion piece 'The Little Girl Found' are, metrically, trochaic versions of the first part of Wesley's stanza in 'Rejoice, the Lord is King' or of John Byrom's 'My spirit longs for thee'. 'The Lamb' is printed as three stanzas, each one different, in Keynes' edition;[1] but if stanzas 2 and 3 are combined, and the lines are indented as in stanza 1, the whole poem

---

[1] *The Complete Writings of William Blake*, ed. Geoffrey Keynes. 1966 edn., p. 115.

becomes one composed of two identical stanzas, each with ten three- or four-stress lines; and then each may easily be seen as a much expanded version of the common hymnodic "Short Metre". Next comes 'The Blossom'; and here one encounters something of a surprise. Replace an iambic by a trochaic rhythm, and the stanza of the poem is the same (save for being one line short in the second half) as the stanza-form of doubtless the best-known of all eighteenth-century hymns: 'God Save the King'. (It was not, presumably, this particular example of the form which most endeared itself to Blake.)

The next poem in the collection is 'The Ecchoing Green':

> The Sun does arise,
> And make happy the skies;
> The merry bells ring
> To welcome the Spring . . .

But suppose that the poem is rearranged to print two lines as one:

> The Sun does arise, and make happy the skies;

—and so on. There is then a very clear similarity to a well-known near-contemporary hymn by Reginald Heber:

> Brightest and best of the sons of the morning,
> Dawn on our darkness and lend us thine aid . . .

and it has really no significance that Heber's stanza is four lines long, while Blake's, if re-printed in this way, would be five.

Next come 'The Divine Image', in hymnal Common Metre, and 'The Chimney Sweep', an anapaestic version (rarely used in hymns) of Long Metre. 'Infant Joy', the next poem, looks little, metrically speaking, like a hymn:

> "I have no name:
> "I am but two days old."
> What shall I call thee?
> "I happy am,
> Joy is my name."
> Sweet joy befall thee!

But in fact, this is one of the poems nearest to hymn metre, and indeed to the most usual one, Common Metre, at that. Blake has simply re-set, and in doing so of course brought out the particular rhythms of, the following Common-Metre stanza:

"I have no name: I am but two
        Days old." What shall I call thee?
"I happy am, Joy is my name."
        Sweét jóy befáll thee!

The next poem, 'The Shepherd', is in four-line triple rhythm. 'Night',
which follows it, is metrically most unusual and striking among the
lyrics. Here is stanza 5 of the poem:

        And there the lion's ruddy eyes
        Shall flow with tears of gold,
        And pitying the tender cries,
        And walking round the fold,
                Saying "Wrath in his meekness,
                "And by his health, sickness
                "Is driven away
                "From our immortal day."

But this is a variant of the old "Proper Metre", as in Doddridge's Hymn
100, which begins:

        Amazing beauteous change:
        A world created new!

—and of course it is at once clear that in this particular case, substance as
well as metre may be to the point. Here is stanza 5 of Doddridge's hymn:

        The tyrants of the plain
        Their savage chase give o'er:
        No more they rend the slain,
        And thirst for blood no more:
                But infant hands
                Fierce tigers stroke,
                And lions yoke
                In flowery bands.

Next comes 'A Cradle Song', basically in Long Metre (with stanzas of
four four-stress lines); and 'The Little Boy Lost', 'The Little Boy Found',
and 'Nurse's Song', which are all close to Common Metre, though in
the last of these Blake's triple rhythms are insistent. The seven-stress
lines of 'Holy Thursday' ("'Twas on a Holy Thursday, their innocent
faces clean" and so on) of course mean that each two lines of the poem
make a four-line stanza in Common Metre.

After this comes 'On Another's Sorrow':

> Can I see another's woe,
> And not be in sorrow too?
> Can I see another's grief,
> And not seek for kind relief? . . .

This, in both metre and rhyme, is again identical with hymns like Wesley's 'Jesu, lover of my soul':

> Jesu, lover of my soul,
> Let me to Thy bosom fly,
> While the nearer waters roll
> While the tempest still is high . . .

At first glance the next poem, 'Spring', seems quite remote from hymnody:

> Sound the flute!
> Now it's mute.
> Birds delight
> Day and Night;
> Nightingale
> In the dale,
> Lark in sky,
> Merrily,
> Merrily, merrily, to welcome in the year.

But leave aside the refrain (which echoes Shakespeare's "Merrily, merrily, shall I live now,/Under the blossom that hangs on the bough"), and one eighteenth-century hymn, at any rate, is remarkably close—in more, once again, than metre only. It is by John Newton, and its first stanza is printed below in eight lines instead of the usual four:

> Kindly spring
> Again is here,
> Trees and fields
> In bloom appear;
> Hark! the birds
> In artless lays
> Warble their
> Creator's praise.

If we append Blake's refrain to this, we could slip the whole nine lines (though I am far from claiming the result as an embellishment) into Blake's poem.

Besides 'The Voice of the Ancient Bard', which has already been

referred to, only three poems remain. 'The School Boy' is in Common
Metre with an extra (fifth) three stress-line at the end of the stanza; it
must be admitted that the rhythms of this poem are somewhat distinctive, with many free deviations from its own basic pattern. 'Laughing
Song' is in Long Metre, but triple instead of double rhythm:

> When the green woods laugh with the voice of joy . . .

—and 'The Little Black Boy', which begins:

> My mother bore me in the southern wild . . .

is in exactly the metre of such well-known hymns as 'Abide With Me'
(though this particular example of the metre was composed after Blake
had written his poem).

This short review of *Songs of Innocence* in the context of hymn-metres
therefore reaches a striking conclusion. Metrically, these lyrics make as
clear a parallel with eighteenth-century hymns, as they make a contrast
with eighteenth-century lyric (such as it was) viewed as a whole. Nor
should one think for a moment that if one admits such licences and
deviations as I have noted from time to time, or allows stanzas to be
re-set as I re-set 'Infant Joy' or 'Spring', in order to bring out their
metrical affinities, anything may then be made to look like anything. A
few minutes' attempt to do for Donne's lyrics, say, or for Herbert's,
what has been done here for Blake's, will suffice to show that their cases
are totally different. To relate their work to hymn-metre in anything like
the same way is simply out of the question.

But if the continuity between Blake's lyrics, and the hymns of his
time, is to be taken any further than this, we must have regard not to the
hymns in general, but now to one kind in particular: the hymn for
children. *Songs of Innocence* is a collection of poems written, as Blake says
in the introductory poem, so that "every child may joy to hear". But
while other or earlier writers use the preposition "for" (Mrs. Barbauld,
Hymns in Prose for Children, 1787; Christopher Smart, *Hymns for the
Amusement of Children*, 1775; Charles Wesley, *Hymns for Children*, 1763;
Isaac Watts, *Divine and Moral Songs for the Use of Children*: the first of
many editions was dated 1715) Blake's preposition is "of". This detail
has a surprising relevance, and I shall return to it.

Hymns were usually based upon a verse in the Bible; and this is so
much a part of them that one may reasonably ask for proof that (so far as
content is concerned) hymnodic influence is more than simply Biblical

influence, with some hymn as mere jejune intermediary. The answer is that while the spirit and tone of all true hymns must naturally go back to something somewhere in scripture, it need not go back overmuch to the verse in scripture which the author gives as ostensible source. One example will make this clear. Philip Doddridge's 'The swift declining day ...' is a straightforward evensong hymn which celebrates, literally, and in a more or less idyllic mode, the fall of night. The reference is to *Jeremiah* xiii, 16. But one's surprise that anything idyllic could be referred to that intimidating prophet is immediately justified if the reference is consulted: "Give glory to the Lord your God, before he cause darkness ... and while ye look for light, he turn it into the shadow of death." Taken as a whole, what Jeremiah wrote is *anti*-idyllic; his concern, predictably, is with the spiritual darkness of a God-cursed country. Doddridge's reference to him is really quite nominal: a convenient scriptural warrant for composing something along quite other lines.

Blake has no corresponding poem in *Songs of Innocence*; but in *Poetical Sketches*, 'To the Evening Star' is already, so far as its content goes, something by way of an evening hymn. One idea in it is remarkable. The star is the "angel of the evening" that is to ". . . smile upon our evening bed", an idea developed in "night" (ll. 23–4) and in 'A Cradle Song' (l. 5). For angels to watch over the sleeper now seems a familiar idea, and it comes in hymns like Heber's 'God that madest earth and heaven', or 'Saviour, breathe an evening blessing', by Edmeston and Bickersteth. But both of these are later than Blake. The folk rhyme:

> Matthew, Mark, Luke and John
> Bless the bed that I lie on;
> There are four corners to my bed
> Which four angels overspread ...

is earlier than Blake: one version is recorded by John Aubrey. But before Blake, this particular concept of angel watchfulness is decidedly uncommon. On the other hand, it is clear in Watts's 'An Evening Hymn' in his *Divine and Moral Songs for the Use of Children*; this opens with the words, "Let angels guard my head".

This is something of a special reason for linking 'To the Evening Star' with Watts's hymn; and it is inevitable that at this point the whole train of thought should begin to open out, until one sees the broad and complex pattern in which Blake's lyrics have a place. 'To the Evening

Star' is followed by 'To Morning', a companion piece which might have been called 'To the Morning Star', for it begins:

> O holy virgin! clad in purest white
> Unlock heav'n's golden gates.

In setting the two pieces side by side, Blake was conforming to a well-established convention. Smart, Wesley (in his *Hymns for Children*) and Watts all include such a pair in their collections. It must also be (unless he duplicated it independently) from Watts's 'Morning Song' that Blake got the phrase "the chambers of the east", which he uses in both 'To Morning' and 'To the Muses' (the Biblical source, as I said earlier, is *Psalms* xix, 5). But behind Watts there stands another whose work was of the greatest importance for Blake: Bunyan. Bunyan's *A Book for Boys and Girls* (the stress on verse for children is always present in this tradition), first appeared in 1686. From 1724, when the ninth edition was published, it was called 'Divine Emblems'; and were the present discussion intended to clarify literary history in general, not equip one simply for a fuller awareness of Blake, there would be much to say about the link between these children's hymns, and the tradition of religious emblem-poetry which in England goes back for a hundred years before Bunyan.

Within the children's hymns, continuities that run forward to Blake are sometimes quite straightforward, even verbal; but one regularly notices that although a biblical source may be the ultimate source, it is changed in meaning or in tone before it reaches Blake. In *Amos* iv, 13, we find: "Lo, he that formeth the mountains, and createth the wind . . . and maketh the morning darkness . . . the Lord The God of hosts, is his name." Improbable as it may seem, this is in one sense the point of origin of Blake's lines in 'The Tyger' (where, of course, the idea that God "createth" is also strong):

> When the stars threw down their spears,
> And water'd heaven with their tears,
> Did he smile his work to see? . . .

The connexion seems entirely unreal until Doddridge's Hymn 156 is considered as intermediary. This makes the equation of stars and rebel angels quite explicit:

> . . . *stars and angels* from their seats
> Are by his thunder hurl'd

But more than this, the real point is that Doddridge's hymn makes an explicit reference back to the passage in *Amos*. Similarly Blake's

> . . . Holy Word . . .
>
> That might control
> The starry pole,
> And fallen, fallen light renew!
>
> O Earth, O Earth return!
> Arise from out the dewy grass;
> Night is worn
> And the morn
> Rises from the slumb'rous mass.

cannot easily be linked in direct fashion to "I am . . . the bright and morning star" of *Revelations* XXII, 16; but it seems much closer to Doddridge's

> Fair Morning star, arise . . .
> The horrid gloom is fled (Hymn 359)

which the author himself refers simply to that verse.[1]

These examples do not throw much direct light on Blake's lyric from the standpoint of their quality as poetry: they are telling in a more general way. They help to show how the children's hymns have genuinely permeated his work, and may turn up anywhere in it; and this fact is important when the question arises of how much weight one should put on the continuity, once one turns from "influences" to interpretation. Another such link runs from Watts's 'Innocent Play' (where the children play along with the "young lambs sporting . . . with fleece so clear and so white") forward to Blake's 'The Lamb'. But the interest quickens when the difference between what is in Blake and what is in his predecessor does not simply happen to be a mere incompleteness of resemblance, but looks like the product of choice—of considered and intended difference on Blake's part.

I am unsure whether my first example will carry conviction: but if by now one can take it as fairly clear that Blake was familiar with Watts's *Songs* (and it will become clearer yet), then there is something full of meaning in the way that the latter's 'Cradle Hymn' differs from 'A Cradle Song' in *Songs of Innocence*. Watts's piece is a lullaby, but as a lullaby it is a good deal open to question. Watts's main interest when

[1] *Works*, Vol. III, p. 632.

writing it seems to have fallen quite outside the lullaby situation. In fact,
'Cradle Hymn' recites the story of the crucifixion, and in its indignation
at the facts, nearly wakes the baby:

> Soft my child, I did not chide thee,
> Though my song might sound too hard . . .
> . . . to read the shameful story
> Makes me angry while I sing.

But Blake's poem is a celebration, not a recitation. It recalls only the
infant Christ, and the only trace of how Watts's child nearly woke up
comes—if trace it is—in the lines:

> Sweet moans, dovelike sighs,
> Chase not slumber from thy eyes.

Quite probably Blake would have thought of a half-waking child without any cue from Watts's piece.

But while in this case Blake's possible transformation of what he found
in an earlier writer is shadowy enough to be attributable to mere chance,
in other cases it is clear that he was writing what was a genuine if implicit
retort to what came before him. His poems need to be seen as taking part
in—or rather, as initiating—a debate.

Here is Bunyan's divine emblem 'Upon the Pismire' (based, of course,
upon *Proverbs* VI, 6: "Go to the ant, thou sluggard; consider her ways,
and be wise"):

> Must we unto the pismire go to school,
>   To learn of her in summer to provide
> For winter next ensuing? Man's a fool,
>   Or silly ants would not be made his guide.
> But sluggard, is it not a shame for thee
>   To be outdone by pismires? Pr'ythee hear:
> Their works, too, will thy condemnation be
>   When at the judgment-seat thou shalt appear.
> But since thy God doth bid to her to go
>   Obey, her ways consider, and be wise;
> The piss-ant tell thee will what thou must do,
>   And set the way to life before thine eyes.

Watts made two pieces on the theme of Bunyan's single one. First there
is 'The Ant', in which he observes merely in passing that the "sluggard"
could learn from that assiduous insect. Second comes 'The Voice of the
Sluggard', who sleeps long in bed in the morning, as a result of which the
poet can regretfully begin his second verse:

> I pass'd by his garden, and saw the wild brier,
> The thorn and the thistle grow higher and higher.

But there is a sense in which Watts's two poems become three, or even four, in Blake. First, Blake has a poem in *Songs of Experience* about visiting a garden, which in this context springs an ugly surprise on the reader:

> I went to the Garden of Love,
> And saw what I never had seen:
> A Chapel was built in the midst,
> Where I used to play on the green.
>
> And the gates of this Chapel were shut,
> And "Thou shalt not" writ over the door;
> So I turn'd to the Garden of Love
> That so many sweet flowers bore;
>
> And I saw it was filled with graves,
> And tomb-stones where flowers should be;
> And Priests in black gowns were walking their rounds,
> And binding with briars my joys & desires.

'The Garden of Love' is a garden of idleness and play. It is spoiled not by sluggardliness but by repressive chapel-building priests. The "briars" in it do not belong to the lazy: they are dragooned into use by evil busyness. Second, the theme of the sluggard is implicitly taken up in 'The School Boy':

> I love to rise in a summer morn

the boy says: but he loves to rise to play, not to gloom and oppression at school. The closing stanzas emphatically justify him. In effect the poem is saying that, given what men make of life, sluggards are right.

Third, it seems not unreasonable to take Blake's 'Nurse's Song' as a sort of palinode to the sluggard of Bunyan and Watts. In this poem it is evening not morning; the children are sluggards not because they delay away from work, in bed, but because they delay, away from their beds, at play; and not those who delay, but those who call them from delay, are converted, and sing as they change their minds:

> Well, well, go and play till the light fades away
> And *then* go home to bed.

In all these lyrics, Blake has something to say about sluggards, about those who play and are idle; and what he says is the opposite of what was said before him.

But the fullest use, and the most sharply-defined, that Blake made of the ant and the sluggard, comes in 'A Dream':

> Once a dream did weave a shade
> O'er my Angel-guarded bed,
> That an Emmet lost its way
> Where on grass methought I lay.
>
> Troubled, 'wilder'd, and forlorn,
> Dark, benighted, travel-worn,
> Over many a tangled spray,
> All heart-broke I heard her say:
>
> "O, my children! do they cry?
> "Do they hear their father sigh?
> "Now they look abroad to see:
> "Now return and weep for me."
>
> Pitying, I drop'd a tear;
> But I saw a glow-worm near,
> Who replied: "What ailing wight
> "Calls the watchman of the night?
>
> "I am set to light the ground,
> "While the beetle goes his round:
> "Follow now the beetle's hum;
> "Little wanderer, hie thee home."

Bateson is probably wrong to interpret "weave a shade" in l. 1 simply as "cast a gloom":[1] the phrase should be compared with the sweet dreams that "form a shade" in 'A Cradle Song', and the encouragement in Blake's 'Dream' then comes out all the more clearly. Encouragement, because ultimately the poem implies that the creatures of this world have something more effective than ant-hood, than their own small efforts, to rely on. The point of the poem is that all the ant's striving and effort *do it no good*. Something has to set the "way of life"—we recall Bunyan's phrase—before *its* eyes; and that something (in the first place anyhow) is actually the glow-worm, which does nothing but sit and shine! And the full point is that the glow-worm can say:

> I am *set* to light the ground . . .

The glow-worm is God's own sluggard; and it comes, in its compassion,

[1] *Op. cit.*, p. 121.

to the rescue of God's busybodies. Blake has set "consider the lilies of the field . . ." over the verse from *Proverbs*. Now one sees the point of the first stanza of 'A Dream'. "Where *on grass* methought I *lay*" ("methought" means "in the dream") shows the poet as already following the glow-worm's lead, not the ant's. The wisdom of the poem comes to him in pastoral innocence and idleness. Nor is this fortuitous luck. What has charge of the glow-worm's idle tranquillity has charge also of his: his bed too is "angel-guarded".

Doubtless—or at least possibly—it is no reflection on Christianity, but only on the human fallibility of those who attempt to subscribe to it, that some expressions of Christian piety in verse strike one as distasteful. Bunyan's 'Upon a Snail' seems to me among these:

> She goes but softly, but she goeth sure
> . . .
> She makes no noise, but stilly seizeth on
>   The flower or herb appointed for her food,
> The which she quietly doth feed upon
> . . .
> And though she doth but very softly go,
>   However, 'tis not fast nor slow, but sure;

Watts has nothing about the snail, but for Blake his 'The Rose' seems to have joined company with it. Bunyan's 'The Rose' is a "moral" song rather than a "divine" one, and it simply applies the transience of the rose (which will "wither and die in a day") to human life:

> So frail is the youth and the beauty of man. . . .

In view of this, the hymn concludes, we should devote ourselves to virtue not pleasure: a conventional "Thou Shalt Not" over the door.

Blake has two celebrated poems in *Songs of Experience* which ought to be seen as retorting at these pieces by Bunyan and Watts, and at the Uriah Heep sentiments at least of the former. In 'The Sick Rose', Bunyan's parable is reversed:

> O Rose, thou art sick!
> The invisible worm
> That flies in the night,
> In the howling storm,
>
> Has found out thy bed
> Of crimson joy:
> And his dark secret love
> Does thy life destroy.

Blake has sensed that if religion is the snail eating the flower, it is a plain enemy to life; and this is what his poem says of it. The "worm" we can therefore see not simply as the worm of death, but also, and indeed much more, as a representation of how the divine spirit is conventionally, and disastrously, understood or rather travestied. This, of course, is why the worm is "invisible", and also why it "flies in the night, in the howling storm": there is a hint of *Genesis* I (the Spirit of God moving in darkness on the waters of the primal chaos), of *Job* xxxvi and xxxvii ("With clouds he covereth the light . . . hear attentively the noise of his voice . . . he directeth . . . his lightning unto the ends of the earth. After it a voice roareth: he thundereth . . ."), and perhaps of Jesus asleep in the storm at sea in *Matthew* viii.

The other poem is 'Ah! Sunflower':

> Ah, Sun-flower, weary of time,
> Who countest the steps of the Sun,
> Seeking after that sweet golden clime
> Where the traveller's journey is done:
>
> Where the Youth pined away with desire,
> And the pale Virgin shrouded in snow
> Arise from their graves, and aspire
> Where my Sun-flower wishes to go.

'Ah! Sunflower' relates directly to Watts's 'The Rose', and it calls to mind Lawrence's account of tragedy as "a great big kick at misery". It is a categoric repudiation of wretched if edifying despondency about transience, whether in flowers or in men and women. In either case (Blake contrives to assert), the truth is otherwise; both, all, have "immortal longings" or rather immortal potentialities. Here is their true nature. Neither—and one sees the literal and figurative significance interacting at this very point—need bow the head before a morality of decay and drooping conformism. Both, equally, "arise" and "aspire": death-like deprivation ("*pined away* with desire", ". . . virgin *shrouded* in snow") is not the law of life, but what in due course the law of life will obliterate. Bunyan, Watts, are confuted.

The last poem which calls for detailed attention in this context is 'The Tyger':

> Tyger! Tyger! burning bright
> In the forests of the night,
> What immortal hand or eye
> Could frame thy fearful symmetry?

In what distant deeps or skies
Burnt the fire of thine eyes?
On what wings dare he aspire?
What the hand dare sieze the fire?

And what shoulder, & what art,
Could twist the sinews of thy heart?
And when thy heart began to beat,
What dread hand? & what dread feet?

What the hammer? what the chain?
In what furnace was thy brain?
What the anvil? what dread grasp
Dare its deadly terrors clasp?

When the stars threw down their spears,
And water'd heaven with their tears,
Did he smile his work to see?
Did he who made the Lamb make thee?

Tyger! Tyger! burning bright
In the forests of the night,
What immortal hand or eye
Dare frame thy fearful symmetry?

No one, probably, fails to sense that the penultimate verse of this poem is somehow intrinsic to its whole effect; as also, that the stars in the dark sky, and the "tyger" burning in the dark forest, are somehow one; and that those same stars, which gave up their battle and fell into grief, are one as well with the rebel angels. But what has the tiger really to do with Satan or his host? The poem may be taken back ultimately to *Revelations* XXII, 16, where Christ says, "I am the bright and morning star". Since Satan was also identified with the morning star (cf. *Isaiah* XIV, 12), the passage has a curious ambiguity; though its link with an ambiguity, or at least a two-sidedness, central to Christianity, is doubtless accidental. Watts has one hymn which gives as reference *Job* XXXV, 22: "With God is terrible majesty". "Great God how terrible thou art" it begins. Its most memorable line is

> God is a bright and burning fire.

One senses, I believe, a nearness already to Blake's poem, but Watts's hymn goes on:

> his *eye*
> *Burns* with *immortal* jealousy

By now the conclusion, surprising as it is, cannot be missed. It becomes impossible not to believe that when he wrote his poem about the terrors of the tiger, Blake had in mind Watts's piece on the terrors of God.

In the final version of the poem, as against the drafts of it in the 1793 *Notebook*, Blake altered the line "Did he who made the lamb make thee?", and turned "lamb" into "Lamb". It was no matter of mere eighteenth-century capitalization; and if it is said that this merely matches the capital for "Tyger", one has to say that that clinches the point. The tiger in the poem is no simple creation of the deity; he *is* the deity: if God is what the pundits have said, if he could have seen the Fall of the angels he himself made, and viewed this benignly, as he viewed each day's work of creation, then God is himself a tiger. Just as there is a question to answer, how could one God have created both the tiger and the lamb, so (the poem implies) there is a prior question: what "immortal hand or eye" could have created—or to put the question more literally, how could there be—a God who is at once a God of love, and one of terrible jealousy?—a "Tyger" and a "Lamb"? In this poem also, Blake is continuing the hymn tradition, and at the same time inverting it and challenging it. Contrary to his predecessors, he saw—or perhaps one should say supposed—that the God-of-Love-God-of-Terror formula was not a sacred mystery of religion, but a stupefying fraud.

At this point, surely, one cannot but revert to Blake's distinctive preposition: Songs *of* Innocence, where all his predecessors wrote songs *for* children; and one can see the force and newness of the closing lines of his introductory poem:

> And I wrote my *happy* songs
> Every child may *joy* to hear.

Or one may put this another way. Blake, in *Songs of Innocence*, was writings songs such that, in a sense, they could come spontaneously from children; the others were arranging an adult vision and an adult morality in such a form as might be imposed down upon them. A poem in another vein, written at almost exactly the time when Blake was writing *Poetical Sketches*, sums up this matter neatly. I suppose it is inoffensive enough, in its way: though not if one's values are Blake's (and certainly not, if one knows what sort of art children can produce of their own). It closes the second volume of George Keate's *Poetical Works*, published in 1781:

ADVICE TO A LITTLE GIRL
The Author's Daughter,

On her being honored with some instruction

By Mrs. DELANY

In cutting out paper.
Written at Bulstrode,
M.DCC.LXXX

With that Benevolence which condescends
    To glide its Knowledge to the youthful Heart,
O'er thee, my Child, the Good Delany bends,
    Directs thy Scissars, and reveals her Art.

Ah! seize the happy Moment!—She can shew
    The mazy Path mysterious Nature treads;
Can steal her varied Grace, her varied Glow,
    And all the changeful Beauties that she spreads.

Then mark thy kind Instructress, watch her Hand,
    Her Judgment, her inspiring Touch attain;
Thy Scissars, make like her's, a Magic Wand!—
    Tho' much I fear thy Efforts will be vain.—

Failing in this, my Child, forbear the Strife;
    Another Path to Fame by her is shown;—
Try by the Pattern of her honor'd Life,
    With equal Virtue to cut out thine own.

The well-meant condescension, and the note of moral exhortation, are inescapable; and so they are in the children's verses of Blake's predecessors. Even Watts was no exception. In his 'An Evening Song', the angels guard the child's bed while he sings

But how my childhood runs to waste,
    My sins how great their sum!

Elsewhere we find Watts's child characterizing himself as

By nature, and by practice too,
    A wretched slave to sin.

If even this is not damning enough, Watts supplies what is missing:

> There is a dreadful hell,
> And everlasting pains
> There sinners must with devils dwell
> In darkness, fire, and chains . . .
>
> Great God, how terrible art thou
> To sinners ne'er so young.

One is tempted to ask what is the precise sense of the title '. . . Songs for the Use of Children': are children the users or the used? Wesley, who condemned Watts's hymns for descending to the level of the child's intellect, produced his *Hymns for Children* in 1763. He invites his youthful singers to rollick through passages like the following:

> O Father, I am but a child,
> My body is made of the earth,
> My nature, alas! is defiled,
> And a sinner I was from my birth.

This is from Wesley's '*Hymns for the Youngest*': the rather unusual metre is exactly reproduced in Blake's 'The Shepherd':

> How sweet is the shepherd's sweet lot! . . .

But there is a difference of sentiment. Blake's "joy", in fact, comes all the time to mind: it is the paralysing *joylessness* of so many of the children's hymns—not, as will transpire, of all—that surprises a reader today. Christopher Smart's *Hymns for the Amusement of Children* (1775) often invite the same response. Here are some lines from 'Beauty: for a Damsel':

> It is not so—my features are
> Much meaner than the rest;
> A glow-worm cannot be a star,
> And I am plain at best.

Perhaps the point may be put simply: in the world of *Songs of Innocence*, a glow-worm *was* a star.

But sin-filled joylessness was not the only note struck by these authors. To suggest that would be wholly unfair to them. Here are two short lyrics from Smart's collection that have quite a different quality, and it is a quality to some extent reminiscent of the *Songs of Innocence*:

D

Mirth

If you are merry sing away,
    And touch the organs sweet;
This is the Lord's triumphant day,
Ye children in the gall'ries gay,
    Shout from each goodly seat.

It shall be May to-morrow's morn,
    A field then let us run,
And deck us in the blooming thorn,
Soon as the cock begins to warn,
    And long before the sun.

I give the praise to Christ alone,
    My pinks already shew;
And my streak'd roses fully blown,
The sweetness of the Lord make known.
    And to his glory grow.

Ye little prattlers that repair
    For cowslips in the mead,
Of those exulting colts beware,
But blythe security is there,
    Where skipping lambkins feed.

With white and crimson laughs the sky,
    With birds the hedge-rows ring;
To give the praise to God most high,
And all the sulky fiends defy,
    Is a most joyful thing.

For Saturday

Now's the time for mirth and play,
Saturday's an holiday;
Praise to heav'n unceasing yield,
I've found a lark's nest in the field.

A lark's nest, then your play-mate begs
You'd spare herself and speckled eggs;
Soon she shall ascend and sing
Your praises to th' eternal King.

These verses, and the on the whole carefree (if technically wretched) wood-

cut of children at play that accompanied the second of them, bring Smart nearer to Blake, and remind one of Smart's wholly other, and rapturously life-affirming verse.

Wesley, in "Lamb of God I look to thee", can let his children sing:

> Loving Jesus, gentle Lamb,
> In Thy gracious hands I am;
> Make me, Saviour, what thou art.

Watts's children, as they take up his "I sing the almighty power of God", do not have to think of his tigrish power, his "terrible majesty", but of how glow-worms are, in a sense, stars:

> There's not a plant or flower below
> But makes Thy glories known.

Most of all, one finds this other note in Doddridge's hymns. There is No. 111:

> Array'd in beardless green
>   The hills and valleys shine,
> And man and beast is fed
>   By Providence divine.

I have already quoted Doddridge's hymn 100, which refers to the "amazing beauteous change" of the Apocalypse:

> . . . infant hands
> Fierce tigers stroke
> And lions yoke
> In flowery bands.

When Doddridge writes in this hymn of the transformation that is to come upon the earth, he certainly points the way forward to Blake, and it is the Blake of *Songs of Innocence* as well as of Night 9 of *Vala* or the closing sections of *Jerusalem*. There is also the innocent pastoral side to Doddridge's hymns viewed generally: as in No. 208, 'Ye little flock whom Jesus feeds'.

What then distinguishes Blake from these others? It is that he retains the pastoral and beatific side of their religious feelings, while he totally repudiates the sin-and-retribution side—turns it, indeed, into the very hall-mark of evil. That this is his startling transformation of the tradition, and the logic-of-argument behind a number of seeming-innocent *Songs of Innocence*, does not by now need further elaboration. What remains to be explored is how these facts created something distinctive, and in a sense profound, in the positive side of Blake's vision.

Doddridge's *Hymns* are of course much more numerous than the poems in this single collection of Blake's: and something which is true of *Songs of Innocence* is in one way more easily noticed in the *Hymns* than in the *Songs*. Doddridge's spiritual allegiance to the Old Testament determines his imagery; and it is not only a recurrent imagery, but an imagery very distinctive in its quality, and what might be called *self-completing* in its structure. By this I mean that, taken in all their variety, the images of these hymns suggest not merely a number of different experiences, but a structure of experience that is complete in itself. Night and day, mountain, stream and river, storm and harvest, corn, sheep and the worm, gold and the vine, courts and servants, fire and the trumpet—all this is no miscellany, but the outline of a recognizable society and way of life.

In quite large part, what unifies *Songs of Innocence*, and makes it so different as a collection from *Poetical Sketches*, is that something like this kind of pastoral imagery pervades it too. Field insect, sheep and wild beast; hill and valley meadow; tree and flower and bird; river and wind; night and sunrise are ideas that recur throughout. I am not going to suggest that unity comes through their mere aggregation alone, and in the next chapter I shall discuss the very remarkable kind of unity which, in several cases, seems to run between the images that make up some of the poems. But even as mere aggregation, the imagery in Blake is remarkable. Almost without exception, the poems seem to be about the same landscape, the same "world": it is far from a realistic representation of rural Southern England in the eighteenth century, though perhaps it is one aspect of that, considered and brought to a focus.

But its distinctiveness is much greater than I have yet brought out.
True, in the world of *Songs of Innocence*:

> The Sun doth arise,
> And make happy the skies . . .

for the happy innocence of childhood. But by contrast with what might
be called nymph-and-swain pastoralism, the children are not happy by
themselves, and over and over again are not even seen by themselves.
The world of the *Songs* is a world of childhood in its relation to parent-
hood ('Infant Joy', 'The Little Boy Lost', 'The Little Boy Found', 'The
Little Black Boy', and stanza 5 of 'The School Boy'), or to the "wise
guardians" of the nurse or the beadle ('Nurse's Song', 'Holy Thursday'—
this poem will be discussed again later), or to the old in general ('The
Ecchoing Green': in this case, Blake's illustration particularly confirms
what is being said by the text). Elsewhere the weak or gentle are suc-
coured and guarded by angels, or by the predator-animals whose pre-
datoriness has been transformed into regal gentleness ('The Little Girl
Lost', 'The Little Girl Found', 'Night'). As 'The Lamb' and 'The
Shepherd' make clear, the question that arises first and naturally about
the lamb is of his maker: and the sheep—which means, one notes, the
lamb and its tender, "replying" mother the ewe—are seen through the
eyes of their guardian.

These things, taken all together, give the collection a unique quality.
Putting the matter in terms of the Old Testament, one may say that Blake
has retained its distinctively *patriarchal* pastoralism, while totally rejecting
everything minatory or punitive that went with that patriarchism; and
that this great change of feeling has been maintained within a substantially unchanged range of sensuous detail and concreteness. Putting the
matter more directly, the *Songs of Innocence* are radiant with innocence of
an extraordinary kind: an innocence that is not partial in experience only,
and innocent because irresponsible, but innocence that is one with tranquillity and experience, with dignity and even wisdom; an innocence,
therefore, that brings with it its own spontaneous order. Here is Blake's
"world created new", in the most literal sense. *Songs of Innocence* is
visionary because it sees not imaginary incidents, but a new and intelligible and precious ideal of totality.

The next chapter will examine the detail of some poems of which this
is most clearly true. But first it will review the rejection of this vision in
Songs of Experience. What will transpire is that the vision of *Innocence*

leads often to one kind of form, and its rejection to quite another kind. I shall then examine Blake's rejection of the *Songs of Experience* vision.

3. *Experience, Involvement, Withdrawal*

Blake's poetry of visionary innocence is his greatest achievement, or at least his most indisputable success. As a collection, there is nothing in our language to set beside *Songs of Innocence*. But to see Blake's work, even up to 1790, solely in terms of those poems would be silly. By now there is no need to refute old-fashioned notions of the eighteenth century as an age of sense, reason and decorum. Those things hold good for no more than one smallish part of eighteenth-century society; and even that only when this part of society is considered by itself, and not as predatory on the rest—which it was. More than this, the later eighteenth century (and earlier nineteenth) was a period of repression, violence, political crisis and widespread suffering probably without parallel in modern England. The Seven Years' War with France was soon followed by the American crisis and War of Independence; and that, by the outbreak of the French Revolution, the war with revolutionary France, and Pitt's savage repression of radicalism at home. As against this, for the first time, many were coming to see society as something like a grand conspiracy of the great and rich against the small and poor, and the victorious heroes of history as not very different from the bloodthirsty pirates of the age itself. Scott's novel *The Pirate* was later to make exactly this point; and Blake's lyrics were written not only in succession to the hymns of Watts and Wesley, but in the very years of the revolutionary writings of Tom Paine, Godwin, and Mary Wollstonecraft.

Already in *Poetical Sketches* it is clear that there is a side of Blake very different indeed from his vision of patriarchal innocence. The *Prologue intended for a Dramatic Piece of King Edward the Fourth* in that collection is clearly an attack on the destructive militarism of a ruling class:

> When Sin claps his broad wings over the battle . . .
> O who can answer at the throne of God?
> The Kings and Nobles of the Land have done it!
> Hear it not, Heaven, thy Ministers have done it!

Erdman has argued that *King Edward the Third* was intended to be, when complete, an attack on the aggression of the French Wars:[1] his case is necessarily inconclusive, but he is quite probably right. *Gwin King of Norway* seems to owe a good deal to Gray's translations from Old Norse poetry like *The Fatal Sisters* and *The Descent of Odin* (it also seems quite possible that, along with other things, Gray's Odin and Lok helped to suggest the names for Blake's Orc and Los in the Prophetic Books). But in this poem Blake struck a new and radical note quite foreign to Gray:

> The Nobles of the land did feed
> Upon the hungry Poor . . .

Besides this, there are several turns of phrase in the poem (such as the likening of Gwin's warriors to *lion's whelps*, and the defiance of Gwin in the words "Thou'rt swept from out the land") which make it possible, anyhow, that Gwin is a substitute for *George*, that what was literary and antiquarian for Gray was something quite other than that for Blake; and that in writing his own poem, Blake was rejoicing in the American War of Independence. Again, the prose fragment 'Then She Bore Pale Desire', written at about the same time as some of the *Poetical Sketches*, is almost a historical 'Progress of Pride', to be read as a riposte to poems like Gray's 'Progress of Poesy' or Thomson's 'Liberty'.

This side of Blake shows also in his 'Marginalia' to the aphorisms of Lavater. These marginalia again date from about 1788.[2] Lavater wrote:

> I know not which I should hate most; the scoffer
> at virtue and religion . . . or the pietist who
> crawls, groans, blubbers, and secretly says to
> gold, thou art my hope! and to his belly, thou
> art my god! [No. 61]

Blake succinctly added "I hate crawlers": he apparently knew which of the two to hate the most. Elsewhere, he found Lavater writing:

> Who begins with severity, in judging of another,
> ends commonly with falsehood . . . [No. 36.]

and he adds:

> False! Severity of judgment is a great virtue.

Certainly it is what we find, and prize, in some of his lyrics of the early 1790's.

[1] Erdman, *op. cit.*, pp. 64 ff.   [2] *Complete Writings*, p. 65.

So it would be quite wrong to see the polemical, radical poems of *Songs of Experience* as something new in Blake. That side was there from the start. On the other hand, something about this polemical radicalism, this "severity of judgement", is unquestionably new: and this something is that Blake can no longer keep his severity of judgment from challenging his vision of innocence. In *Poetical Sketches*, the radical and anti-war pieces seem largely, though not entirely, literary in inspiration. The horrors of war (if not outright condemnation of these) are in Gray's pieces; the sufferings of the common people through the military adventures of their rulers are vivid in Shakespeare's history plays. All these sentiments, indeed, are one part of eighteenth-century literary tradition. Blake's radicalism could draw on these facts, and at this stage, could still remain with something of the abstract and doctrinaire. That could exist in his mind alongside his patriarchal pastoralism. But between the first collection of *Songs* and the second, something happened to give Blake's social feelings a greater immediacy, and make any further such insulation impossible.

This something was less the French Revolution considered simply in itself, than its impact at home in Britain. Bronowski points out[1] how in 1791 the radical bookseller Joseph Johnson (who seems to have become a friend of Blake in the later 1780's) had seen danger ahead, and suddenly abandoned the publication of Paine's *The Rights of Man*. He was wise. The following year saw the Royal Proclamation against Seditious Writings, and Paine and his new printer were soon prosecuted. Paine was later prosecuted in his absence (he had fled abroad) for treason. In July 1791 the Birmingham mob, incited, it is alleged, by the authorities, had sacked the house and laboratory of the radical dissenter Joseph Priestley. There were other attacks on dissenters, and it became clear that the government avoided giving them protection.

As revolution took its course in France, and fears of revolution at home infected with panic the unshakeable assurance of the powers-that-be in their own total rightness, repression went further. In December 1792 a convention of Parliamentary Reformers was held in Edinburgh; the following year one of its leaders, Thomas Muir, was prosecuted for sedition and sentenced to fourteen years' transportation by the notorious Lord Braxfield (it was he who joked, from the bench, that Christ "waur hangit" as an innovator). The following month Thomas Palmer, a respectable Scottish Unitarian minister, and ex-Fellow of a Cambridge

[1] Bronowski, *William Blake* (1954 edn.), p. 68.

college, received a like sentence. Just as the words "every ban" in 'London' (as well, of course, as meaning "curse" which comes later in the poem) may have come into Blake's mind from the repressive Proclamations, so the "mind-forg'd manacles" themselves may not be general and figurative only, but refer also to how respectable men like Muir and Palmer were appearing on trial manacled in court as if they were common felons. Early the next year, three more reformist leaders were sentenced to fourteen years' transportation. The acquittal in London, during the autumn of 1794, of Thomas Hardy and others on charges of high treason, did not reverse the general trend of the time. This continued in the prohibitory Acts of 1795, the suspension of *habeas corpus*, the prosecution and imprisonment of Joseph Johnson and many others, and the Combination Acts of 1799. Hardy was acquitted when the defence showed up the prosecution evidence as lies. But the real significance of the acquittal was to stress how the police spy and the *agent provocateur* were everywhere. Here is the universe of uncertainty and fear that Blake captures in the first stanza of 'London':

> . . . mark in every face I meet
> Marks of weakness, marks of woe.

The opening lines of the poem contrast this with the "charter'd" Thames and the city's chartered streets. But what is in Blake's mind is no generalized contrast between the free and the trammelled life: it is the present and pressing destruction of the political liberty of his fellows and himself. The first draft of stanza 2 makes this clearer still:

> . . . in every voice, in every ban
> The *german* mind-forg'd links I hear.

Blake of course means the House of Hanover with its German troops— used against British settlers in America, and now being stationed across England, ostensibly for action in the French War. Whether Blake changed the line because "links" was inadequate, or "german" seditious, is not easy to say.

Blake's response to these years is clear in a quatrain in the 1793 *Notebook*; again, the proverbial and popular is the form he adopts:

> *An ancient Proverb*
> Remove away that black'ning church:
> Remove away that marriage hearse:
> Remove away that man of blood:
> You'll quite remove the ancient curse.

Clearly, this might have been intended as a final stanza to 'London'. "Man of blood" is a revision of "place of blood", or, as Erdman[1] suggests, "palace . . .". In another version, Blake left a dash. Erdman is wrong, I think, to argue that this proves Blake to have written "palace", not the innocuous "place". His dash may have replaced "man"; which was quite seditious enough, since "thou man of blood", from 2 *Samuel* XVI, 7, meant King David, and therefore in effect meant King George. But what one can say, briefly, is that *Songs of Experience* record Blake's discovery that there is an "ancient curse"—one, that is, under which men have suffered throughout history—and that it calls the whole vision of Innocence in question.

It is helpful to trace the development of this new attitude in one or two of the poems in the 1793 *Notebook*: poems which never found their way into *Songs of Experience*. In the little poem 'Day', for example, the sun, that "made happy the skies" at its rising in 'The Ecchoing Green', and made the birds sing in 'The School Boy', has become an emblem of bloodthirsty war-mongering and regal intemperance:

> The Sun arises in the East,
> Cloth'd in robes of blood and gold;
> Swords and spears and wrath increast
> All around his bosom roll'd,
> Crown'd with warlike fires & raging desires.

("Increast" is possibly an adjective, meaning something like "greater than ever".) Blake is recognizing in these lines how something in his world of radiant innocence may be seen, and perhaps more truthfully, in a disastrously other way. Also in the *Notebook*, revealing and disquieting along the same lines, is 'The wild flower's song'.[2] This short lyric (in the manuscript it appears in two fragments, which are here joined together) has a title, and an opening, that seem right for *Songs of Innocence*. But what as a whole it invites is inclusion in a collection entitled 'Songs of *Disillusion*': which is the point—that is what the *Songs of Experience* in part amount to:

> As I wander'd the forest,
> The green leaves among,
> I heard a wild flower
> Singing a song:

[1] Erdman, *op. cit.*, p. 258.   [2] *Complete Writings*, pp. 175 and 170.

> I slept in the earth
> In the silent night
> I murmur'd my fears
> And I felt delight.
>
> In the morning I went
> As rosy as morn
> To seek for new Joy
> *But I met with scorn*

One can glimpse how Blake is thinking as he composes here. The first version of "wild flower" was "wild thistle": that would have spoilt the stinging surprise of the last line, but it shows clearly how Blake is seeing a new reality in the "green fields and happy groves/Where flocks have took delight". This is the world of 'My pretty Rose Tree', that draws something (as was mentioned in Chapter 1) from the folk-song; but it ends with a dry, sharp irony not perhaps impossible in folk-song, but far from typical of it:

> But my Rose turn'd away with jealousy,
> And her thorns were my only delight.

'A Little Girl Lost' opens with a preliminary stanza that makes the picture clearer:

> Children of the future Age,
> Reading this *indignant* page . . .

Blake is still thinking about lyrics for children: but now they are children with eyes to be opened. The "indignation" that Blake may have found in Watts's lullaby, and almost eradicated when he wrote his own, has come back in a wholly new, non-traditional, and socially conscious form.

"Eyes to be opened" is quite the right phrase.

> "Why of the sheep do you not learn peace?"
> *"Because I don't want you to shear my fleece"*

Blake wrote in the 1793 *Notebook* as 'An answer to the parson'; and again, this can for Blake be no passing thought, for it is a recognition, and an admission, that the vision of *Songs of Innocence* may be not vision but the lack of it. 'Nurse's Song' in *Songs of Experience* is not a particular success among the lyrics, since there is some uncertainty, or at least lack of clarity, in the meaning of its closing lines:

> Your spring and your day are wasted in play,
> And your winter and night in *disguise*.

One can easily give an esoteric neo–Platonist meaning to "disguise":
but if this is its only meaning, the beautiful simplicity and directness of
the best of the 'Songs' is still lacking. In spite of its imperfections, though,
the poem in its opening lines still expresses with great bluntness Blake's
repudiation of "innocence":

> When the voices of children are heard on the green
> And whisp'rings are in the dale,
> The days of my youth rise fresh in my mind,
> My face turns green and pale.

The opening words suggest that the poem is going to be a gentle and
guileless companion-piece to 'Nurse's Song' in *Songs of Innocence*: but
what supervenes is a note of mocking parody, or rather of sarcastic self-
accusation.

It is well known, of course, that a number of poems in *Songs of
Experience* are counterpart-pieces to poems in *Songs of Innocence*. One
pair that has been relatively little discussed is 'The Divine Image' and its
later counterpart 'The Human Abstract'. The first of these is in the
"Common Metre" and simple diction of the hymns, and the virtues that
it celebrates are the traditional Christian ones of ". . . Mercy, Pity, Peace
and Love"; to each of which Collins, for example, had written a conventional eighteenth-century ode. The essential structure of the poem is
an identification of these virtues (which are seen collectively in the poem
as "the good") with both God and man, and therefore the identification
of God *with* man: man *is* "the Divine Image". The poem cannot be
regarded as among the major successes of *Songs of Innocence*, not only
because the visionary quality is absent from it, but also because there is a
sense in which it contains, as it were, the seed of its own refutation. This
is because, by the very neatness of its argumentative form, the poem says
implicitly that man has not only those four virtues, but also the capacity
to think, argue, agree—and so of necessity disagree. Verse of this kind
simply cannot have the closed finality of 'Nurse's Song' or 'The Lamb'
or 'A Dream'.

It is precisely this *exposure to retort* that the *Songs of Experience* poem
exploits:

> Pity would be no more
> If we did not make somebody poor . . .

What the latter poem asserts is that conventional Christian virtues exist as mere froth (or, maybe, mere varnish would be better) on the surface of a society founded not on great virtues, but great evils—poverty, unhappiness, fear, selfishness, cruelty and the 'Raven' of death. Poetically the piece is far richer than its counterpart, for Blake means "summary" by "Abstract" in the title, and the poem's growth is such that the sham virtues and real evils grow out of each other in organic progression until the whole forms a savage parody of the story of the 'Tree of Jesse' (*Isaiah* II, I). Humanity grows through evil veritably to Death itself. There is a third poem in the series: '*A* Divine Image', which Blake did not include in *Songs of Experience*, though he etched it, according to Keynes, in about 1794. In this poem, Blake seems to see a new truth: I shall return to it.

The new vision of *Songs of Experience*—selective, sarcastic, critical—results in a radically new poetic form, new mode of poetic organization. The visionary harmonies of the earlier collection had induced their own characteristic form: intricate, moving, and beautifully distinctive. Of this 'The Lamb' is a clear if simple example, simple because poetic form here merges into explicit statement. The point is that one can virtually assert this poem to have a structure, inasmuch as it has a structure of ideas: and the structure of ideas is a structure of identity, of the merging and inter-fusion which is the ultimate condition of harmonious oneness. In a world of harmony, the work of the Creator tends simply towards being a duplication and re-duplication of himself: until finally, it is oneness which *is* blessedness.

> Little Lamb, who made thee . . .?
> Little Lamb, I'll tell thee:
> He is called by thy name . . .
> He became a little child.
> I a child and thou a lamb
> We are called by his name.
> *Little Lamb, God bless thee!*

The last line in this quotation immediately follows, and seems what necessarily follows, the all-embracing identities which precede it.

The 'Introduction' to *Songs of Innocence* is like this too. The text of this is reproduced in full on pages 28–9. Perhaps the line which leads one most easily into the structure of this poem is:

> And I stain'd the water clear . . .

Some might wish to make an ambiguity out of this: the clear water is *stained*, or the water is stained *clear*. But that sort of verbal ingenuity is what the whole diction and rhythm and narrative line of the poem reject. Yet the impression left with the reader is still of how near the ink and the clear water are together, of how nearly they are one. The staining is a fact in the poem, but it is the water's clarity that is rendered sensuously explicit. Why, however, "the" water? Since this is not quite idiomatic unless there is a reference to water already, the attentive reader's mind searches instinctively backward in the poem. There is nothing explicit but the child's tears; yet since these are the tears of the "laughing" child on the cloud, they are the joyous showers of rain. (Wicksteed makes it quite clear that the reference to tears in this poem has nothing to do with grief.)[1] But if, ultimately, the singer's ink and the child's tears of joy at what he writes down *are one*, we are still not to think that the ink is made directly from the rain. Since the poet "pluck'd a hollow reed" for his pen (which, clearly, he has already done for his pipe: so pipe and pen themselves come together) there is a stream also in the landscape of the poem. But the stream does not enter the poem by inference merely: for just as there is both a metaphorical, or perhaps one should say spiritual, sense in which the child on the cloud is a heavenly presence (is, in fact, the 'Lamb' about which, or whom, he calls for a song), and also a literal or material sense in which joyful tears from the cloud are just refreshing showers of rain, so there is a material sense in which what goes

> Piping down the valleys wild
> Piping songs of pleasant glee

is simply the stream itself: the stream, that is (to make use of a pun, which is not, I think, quite absent from the poem) as "spring" that comes "o'er the eastern hills" to the "listening valleys" as in an earlier piece. Singer and stream are one, and both are one with spring. Poet sings to spiritual presence of the divine; at the same time, different though not different, there is just a springtime landscape, with a babbling stream, the lambs in the meadows beside it, and the fresh rain-bearing clouds above. There is no need now to tot up all the identities which compose the poem. Its manifold of equations issue from, and communicate, a world of harmonious oneness.

'The Ecchoing Green' expresses something of this even in its title. Sun, skies and bells are all happy by virtue of each other; the birds' song is not

[1] Wicksteed, J. H., *Blake's Innocence and Experience* (1928), p. 80.

simply "loud" but they sing "louder" because of the bells; and the Green is an ecchoing green, literally because it resounds with the cries of the children at play, but also by implication in that it reflects the joyfulness spreading everywhere through the scene. Then in the second stanza of the poem, the whole point is that the old people see in the play of the children an "echo" of their own youth, and themselves laugh in echo of the childish gaiety. Finally, the gaily insistent rhythm binds together the first two verses and the last: "ecchoing" becomes one with "darkening", and the darkening green is itself an echo, though not of course an audible one, of the sleep of children and the song-birds (that are "like" them) which is one with the setting sun.

Perhaps the most remarkable poem of this kind is what I am inclined to think is the finest poetic success of all Blake's lyrics: the 'Holy Thursday' poem in *Songs of Innocence*. Since its children are of course charity children, 'Holy Thursday' may reasonably be seen as in the context of such pieces as Watts's 'Praise for Mercies: On the Poor'.

> Where'er I take my walks abroad . . .
> How many children in the street
> Half-naked I behold

or Christopher Smart's 'Pray Remember the Poor':

> I just came by the prison door,
> I gave a penny to the poor,
> Papa did this good deed approve
> And poor Mama cried out for love;
> Whene'er the poor comes to my gate
> Relief I will communicate.

In Smart's favour one should I suppose recall that a penny was worth a shilling or so: but his poem is ridiculous for more than its entanglement over "poor Mama". 'Holy Thursday' is in another world because it totally reverses the movement of attention: not down from above, as so clearly in Watts and Smart, but up from below. The children *are* the life-bearing waters of the city's river, as they flow in streams into its cathedral; they are flowers, not just from their angelic faces, but because Blake's vision has transfigured the red and blue and green of their coloured charity costumes. The river seems to become a fountain from the "high dome of Paul's" as they sing, and their singing grows into the "mighty wind" that (compare 1 *Kings* XIX, 11–12) was prelude to the divine voice. As the fountain rises up to heaven, their lamb-like radiance becomes one with the divine, with the "harmonious thunderings" of the heavenly choirs. Hence the sudden explosive surprise-yet-total-appositeness of the closing:

> Then cherish pity, lest you drive *an angel* from your door.

Blake is sufficiently close to the tradition he so much changes for his poem to go back to a scriptural text: "Suffer the little children to come unto me, and forbid them not; for of such is the kingdom of God" (*Mark* x, 14). Children are one with river, with fountain, with wind ascending to Heaven, with Angels, with the song of angels, and ultimately with the Divine Principle itself.[1]

But the structure of these poems in *Songs of Innocence* has been examined as preliminary to seeing how great, structurally speaking, is the change in a number of the *Songs of Experience*. Nor is it a simple, single change. 'The Fly', for example, might at a careless reading be taken as similar in structure to the 'Innocence' poems above. But the identity which it asserts between fly and man is in no way a fusion and oneness intuited by a kind of visionary power and presented to the reader in the imagery of the poem: it is a more or less clear-cut parallelism insisted on through the poem by a logical argument. There is a special difficulty in this piece, because the lines:

> If . . .
> . . . the want
> Of thought is death

might be taken in something like a Cartesian sense ("cogito ergo sum"), and then (since Blake could not be supposed to be endorsing Descartes), some kind of unfulfilled condition would give an intricate satirical sense to the close of the poem. I do not pursue this because I think it is wrong. By "thought" Blake means, simply "consciousness"; "thoughtless hand" in 1, 3 means "unconscious of what it is doing"; and in the poem's conclusion:

> Then am I
> A happy fly
> If I live
> Or if I die

---

[1] The connexion between 'Holy Thursday', and what is probably Donald Davie's finest poem, 'Under St. Paul's', has so far as I know not been discussed.

there is no implied "which is absurd" in the last line. The stanza means simple, ". . . If I die I am (like) a once happy fly which now is dead". But regardless of simplicity, the form and structure of the poem are logical. Its continuity is a thinking continuity. The opening words of the later stanzas make this inescapable. "For . . . if . . . then" mean, respectively "Because . . . given-the-premises-that . . . therefore". What unifies is the sharp line of an argument strung through the whole piece.

'The Chimney Sweeper' in *Songs of Experience* is much the same. The first two lines present the situation of the black child sweep in the snow: but the rest of the poem is what he says, and its logical structure is perhaps even more sharply articulated than in 'The Fly', and may be expressed " 'because' A, therefore B and C, and *in the same way* 'because' D, therefore E and F". 'The Human Abstract' and 'A Little Boy Lost' are other poems in which logical argument is prominent. 'The Little Vagabond' is nothing more than a catalogue of the consequences which would follow from a conditional proposition which in fact is not fulfilled.

These poems represent something quite new. They have no parallel in *Songs of Innocence*. But there are other poems in the later collection which introduce another new principle of structure, one of quite a different kind. Poetically, these poems seem in general to be more interesting than the directly polemical, argumentative ones; perhaps this is because, as Keats said, "no philosopher ever reached his goal without putting aside [i.e. disregarding] numerous objections", and the unity of a poem which depends upon argument for its unity is likely to seem precarious, challengeable, and superficial. The other principle of structure, which emerges in some of the *Songs of Experience* poems, might be thought at first to be simply a proposition about experience: a mere matter of fact, as Blake sees fact. But when a poet has a belief about experience which is not stated explicitly, but transpires (by inference) in all the relations between such realities as enter his poem, that belief becomes not only one among his beliefs about the world, but veritably the mode of organization of his poem.

This mode of organization, in a number of the poems, is something like the *reverse* of that in *Songs of Innocence*. There, objects began to merge into each other in harmonious oneness: in these poems, it is as if *everything is held back from contact with everything else*. If the poem has a unity, it is that of a sustained negative conviction. Separateness and repulsion pervade it everywhere. It is a sequence of separated, isolated people that Blake passes and observes in 'London':

> . . . *every* cry of *every* man
> . . . *every* Infant's cry of fear

man and child, church and child sweep, palace and soldier, harlot, client
(it may be), child, bride and groom—each is the enemy of its counterpart, each is without live relation to any of the others. The verbs—
"appalls", "runs in blood down", "blasts", "blights" (and the concealed
actions of fearing, cursing and weeping)—all show this same principle at
work. In 'Infant Sorrow', the child is endangered by the world, struggles
against the father, strives against the swaddling bands, sulks against the
mother. In 'A Little Boy Lost' there is first the selfhood of the little boy,
asserted over the bond between him and his father and brothers: and
then the priest who seems to be enemy as much to the parents as the
child. Even between parent and child there is no active relation, only
helpless weeping.

    The 'Introduction' to *Songs of Experience* is another poem that presents
a universe of disjunction and non-relation. Even the initial image of the
divine presence (the 'Holy Word') walking among the trees is an illustration: its essential structure is not unlike that in 'London' of the poet walking among his fellow-Londoners and noticing them one by one. But the
divine presence is calling the soul that has "lapsed" away from it: and
whether it is the divine presence itself or the (divinely inspired) "voice of
the Bard" that is in question, the starry pole that "might" be controlled
but is not, and the "fallen" light that this might renew but does not, are
"lapsed" into disjunction as well. When the "voice of the Bard" speaks,
as it seems to do through the second half of the poem, what it speaks of is
also opposites and unrelateds: the "starry Floor" (of heaven) and "watery
shore", and the morning that "rises from" the "slumbrous mass" of
the darkened earth. More remarkable still, even what the poem calls for
(as against what it unhappily diagnoses), seem to come in similar terms:

> O Earth, O Earth, return!
> Arise from out the dewy grass

The call is presumably to fallen humanity ("fashioned out of clay"), but
that it should be called on to "arise from out" of the ground from which
it was made is something that follows the reiterated movement of the
poem. Similar again is at least the suggestion carried by the closing lines:

> The starry floor,
> The wat'ry shore
> Is giv'n thee till the break of day

If the esoteric, symbolic meaning of the poem be taken into account, this probably means that at the moment of his spiritual rejuvenation, man will repudiate, and be withdrawn from, the world of the senses and move into the intelligible world. But the poet has found means to refer even to this event (which, in his own terms, would be restoration of harmony) along the lines of the poem's recurrent pattern: what is stressed is the break-up of an integration, the seeming cancellation of a bond.

Turn away no more

the last verse opens: what the poem as a whole depicts, and what it mirrors in its own mode of organization, is a world of universal "turn away".

There was to be one further dramatic change in the formal structure of Blake's lyrical writing, a change manifested in the handful of remarkable later lyrics which occur in his *Notebook* of c. 1800–1803. Some of these were printed in Gilchrist's *Life* of Blake in 1863, but there was no complete printing until over a hundred years after the poems were composed. These poems, however, seem also to represent a decisive new stage in Blake's response to experience, and their distinctive form is a reflection of that.

In 1791, the first book of Blake's *French Revolution* was printed for the radical bookseller Joseph Johnson, and the complete poem was stated to be in seven books, of which the other six, already composed, would be printed "in their Order". But those six remaining books were not printed, and have never been located. Probably Blake destroyed them, and even the First Book was printed but never published, the sole surviving copy of it being in all probability a set of page proofs. Bronowski has stressed the importance of these facts:[1] and whether we agree with his suggestion that Blake suppressed this work on account of severe repression and reactionary government in Britain, or with Keynes's that he did so through disillusionment with the French Revolution itself,[2] or think that both are true, the fact remains that the suppression marks something of great importance in Blake's career.

[1] J. Bronowski, *William Blake* (1944): 1955 edn., pp. 67–79.
[2] *Complete Writings*, pp. 887–8.

Wordsworth and Coleridge, as is well known, began in the earliest days of the French Revolution as enthusiastic radicals and near-revolutionaries, and then in the middle 1790s moved towards a wholly other response to experience, a response which, relatively speaking, amounted to a significant withdrawal from involvement with the immediate political issues of their time. Southey's negligible merits as a poet do not make his very similar career altogether irrelevant. Perhaps the tradition of barely considering Blake along with the other major poets of this time grew up during the long period when Wordsworth and Coleridge were revered and widely influential—we may take Arnold's remarks on the former, and Newman's on the latter,[1] as indications—and Blake was almost wholly unknown. But all three can by now be seen together as reflecting, though each in his personal and quite distinctive way, a profoundly significant movement of their time, to which Scott, and indeed Cobbett, ought also to be related. They reflect, in fact, the confirmation of English society as an anti-revolutionary society: one that, among other things, did not accommodate outspoken political involvement and radicalism among its literary élite. When such outspoken radicalism was next to appear, with Byron and Shelley, it was in effect outlawed; and that English society should have taken this turn has had (needless to say) a profound cultural significance right down to the present.

Blake does not seem to have repudiated his radical opinions at all in the same way as Wordsworth and Coleridge; but the fact remains that he withdrew, at least so far as his writing is concerned, from active expression of them and involvement with current issues. Moreover, he may have retained the attitudes of a radical towards social good and evil, but he to a limited extent resembles the other major poets of his time in ceasing to put his trust in radical remedies. A poem like that which begins "Let the brothels of Paris be opened" (in the 1793 Notebook) shows his early disillusionment with the revolutionary leader Lafayette. That which begins "I saw a Monk of Charlemaine" in the Notebook for 1800–1803 records disillusionment of a far deeper kind:

> The hand of vengeance sought the bed
> To which the purple tyrant fled.
> The iron hand crush'd the tyrant's head
> *And became a tyrant in his stead.*

[1] *Essays Critical and Historical* (1873 edn.), Vol. I, pp. 267–8 (in 'The Prospects of the Anglican Church').

> Untill the Tyrant himself relent,
> The Tyrant who first the black bow bent,
> Slaughter shall heap the bloody plain;
> Resistance and war is the tyrant's gain.

This new conviction must be part of what lies behind 'To Tirzah' and also behind the difference between 'The Human Abstract', and 'A Divine Image' (which Blake etched as early as 1794, but did not include in *Songs of Experience* himself).[1]

'*A* Divine Image' must be read along with '*The* Divine Image' in *Songs of Innocence*, and 'The Human Abstract' in *Songs of Experience*; but its pessimism about humanity is an altogether different thing from what one finds in the latter of these poems. 'The Human Abstract' asserts that the conventional Christian virtues like "Mercy, Pity, Peace and Love" are parasitic on evil and bring it about. The "Cruelty, Jealousy, Terror and Secrecy" of 'A Divine Image' are to a considerable degree the opposites, one by one, of those same conventional virtues ("Secrecy" must also be taken with "Mystery" which appears in stanza four of the other poem). In essence the poem is a sardonic attack on the conventional idea of the Christian God, and the line:

> The Human Face a Furnace seal'd

brings to mind the creative fires of 'The Tyger'. The traditional conception of man as made in the image of God is inverted, and a cruel and vicious deity is seen as in the image of "the Human Form Divine". Yet one cannot but find more in the poem also. Whether its foundation is that the terror-God made man in his image, or that man made the idea of a terror-God, man himself remains the image of such a God—either as his creature or as his creator. The poem is such an attack on Christianity as must spring from disillusionment with regard to humanity as well.

'To Tirzah' which Keynes gives in *Songs of Innocence* as "probably added about 1801", ought perhaps to be read with 'The Land of Dreams' in the Pickering Manuscript. There is a sense in which Blake has now become something like an Idealist. "Binding with briars my joys and desires" is now the office of man's mortal and earthly part, deadening and nullifying his awareness—the "closing of the senses" described in, for example, Chapter 9 of *The First Book of Urizen*. "It is Raised a Spiritual Body" the accompanying illustration quotes from I *Corinthians* xv, 44; as for what is of the Earth and "Born of Mortal Birth", the poem

[1] *Complete Writings*, p. 221.

dismisses it with the simple but decisive "What have I to do with thee?".
In 'The Land of Dreams' there is a vision of pastoral beatitude like that of
Songs of Innocence:

> O, what Land is the Land of Dreams?
> What are its Mountains & what are its Streams?
> O Father, I saw my Mother there,
> Among the Lillies by waters fair.
>
> Among the Lambs, clothed in white,
> She walk'd with her Thomas in sweet delight. . . .

But this is not, as (at least implicitly) in *Songs of Innocence*, a vision of the
world of everyday. The world of everyday is now a "Land of unbelief
and fear", and the world of lambs and lilies an unattainable ideal world
on "the other side". Reminiscence of the closing stanzas of Shelley's
'Adonais' is clearly inescapable. The influence of Plato is of course behind
both.

In Blake in fact, as in Plato, a growing sense of an ideal world of
radiant perfection seems to have gone with a growing sense of how evil
in the world of everyday is not a fit object for attack and polemic, for the
simple and decisive reason that attack is futile when it is attack upon
what is of that world's very essence. Perfection is something that
radically and ineluctably has no place in it. 'Mary', also in the Pickering
manuscript of about 1803, and in superficial appearance a rollicking
ballad in broadsheet style, is no conventional account of a maiden's fall.
Mary falls because goodness, whatever means it may adopt in order
to survive, seems inevitably doomed. Mary is hated in her radiant
beauty, and scorned when she tries to recommend herself by modest
plainness.

> "All Faces have envy, sweet Mary, but thine . . ."

The best-known poem in the Pickering Ms., 'Auguries of Innocence',
also gives expression to this sense that there is no way out, that the
opposite of all evil is no better than what it is opposite to:

> The Questioner, who sits so sly,
> Shall never know how to Reply.
> He who replies to Words of Doubt
> Doth put the Light of Knowledge out.

Confusion or conviction are equally valueless: and the impact of the
whole poem (this has not, I think, been much noticed) is that what

innocence "augurs" is no localized and remediable abuse, but corruption everywhere on all hands. Again, that

> . . . there is a Frown of Frowns
> Which you strive to forget in vain

is what we find in another of these poems, 'The Smile': and the all-healing smile from which the poem takes its name is very conspicuously an ideal entity, the subject of a dream.

'The Golden Net' is almost the finest of these later poems: and in it there begins to evolve the new and distinctive form which is the effective embodiment of their vision. The poem is something like a brilliant, sardonic parody of the 'Judgement of Paris' theme: the young traveller sees not the beauties, but the sufferings, of the three weeping virgins that carry the golden net. Yet all that his pity achieves is to imprison him under their net, turn their sorrow to seemingly sadistic pleasure, and replace their sufferings by suffering of his own.

> O when will the morning rise?

the poem ends: the ideal cry irrupts on the inter-locking world of pain of the poem—much like Shelley's

> . . . from which a glorious Phantom may
> Burst, to illumine our tempestuous day

at the close of his 'Sonnet: England in 1819'. But what Blake now registers as his response to reality is a world of *futile action*, a world in which remedy is merely rearrangement of the disease; and the new form in the poem is a form created by a new kind of narrative, counter-pointed, as it were, into self-defeat.

This cyclic form, embodying Blake's by now almost tragic sense of the potentiality of existence, and drawing vitality and tautness from the narrative thread, is plain also in 'The Crystal Cabinet'. This is a poem on something like the same traditional theme as Keats's 'La Belle Dame Sans Merci'. The poet encounters the maiden in the wilds, she brings him into the delights of her private paradise, this suddenly disintegrates, and he finds himself where he was, but with grief substituted for the original carefree joy. Yet Blake's poem, though it employs this traditional narrative *motif*, gives it a quite new force, in that the maiden's private paradise, her "golden cabinet" is in the event not private at all. It is a redeemed vision of the world of everyday:

> Another England there I saw
> Another London with its Tower
> Another Thames & other Hills,
> And another pleasant Surrey bower.

But it is unrealizable: even as the poet "strove to seize the inmost Form" it burst and disintegrated before him.

Kathleen Raine[1] has shown how much there is in 'The Mental Traveller', the most striking and substantial poem in the Pickering Ms., of Plato's conception in the *Politicus* of alternating phases in the world's history, of these as connected with alternating dominance of body and of soul, and of the whole process as symbolized by the birth and rebirth of Dionysus. Enlightening as she is over these preliminary matters, she leaves untouched what is of more account. The same kind of argument applies here as applied in the case of Gillham's discussion of 'The Blossom': the critic's emphasis transforms interest into pleonasm and therefore into boredom. Were 'The Mental Traveller' some mere *résumé* of conceptions with which we can familiarize ourselves in other authors—whether Plato, Thomas Taylor or Yeats—it would be expendable. Poetic greatness is not to be found in such recapitulation, however intriguing or congenial one may find what it recapitulates.

Blake, however, does quite another thing. In the first place, he enriches his narrative until it is a brilliant sensuous glow. The little girl of the poem is no mere "female child body, or matter, whose dominance alternates with spirit, or soul" (as Miss Raine puts it); she

> . . . is all of solid fire
> And gems and gold . . .

Nor can we say simply, of the lines

> . . . who dare touch the frowning form
> His arm is withered *to the root*

that Blake "employs a Hebraic symbol" when he "indicates . . . the processes of human history . . . are not to be arrested or diverted". The interest of these lines is not that they are a cipher for an (I should think) exceptionally questionable historical dogma. In the first place, their interest is in their metaphoric vigour and their narrative directness. Secondly, this vigour and directness are hardly at all to be explained by

---

[1] 'A Traditional Language of Symbols', *The Listener*, October 9th 1958, pp. 559–60.

reference to I *Chronicles* XIV, 7–10, from which what there is here of "Hebraic symbol" must be fetched.

But further, and more important, the interest and quality of the poem surely resides in this: that as we read it, an impression emerges from it which quite dwarfs and renders insignificant any sense that "here [Blake] follows the teaching of Plato" about gyres; and this impression is, that through his narrative, seemingly at a great distance from every-day reality, Blake has in fact found means to record some of his findings about that reality, and to do so with almost terrifying fulness, directness and sombre force:

> he rends up his manacles
> And binds her down for his delight;
>
> He plants himself in all her Nerves,
> Just as a Husbandman his mould;
> And she becomes his dwelling place
> And Garden fruitful seventy fold.

If we could bring ourselves to use Mr. Gillham's phraseology,[1] we should say that this is about "sexual intimacy" as well as about Miss Raine's (or Plato's) "perpetual alternation of ages": though it so far exceeds Mr. Gillham's notion of these matters as to make "the experience" sound "most distressing" and "very wonderful" all at once. Blake knows more, and has more to say also about other of its potentialities; as well, much more generally, as about what man (or woman) has done to man:

> Her fingers number every Nerve,
> Just as a Miser counts his gold;
> She lives upon his shrieks and cries,
> And she grows young as he grows old.

Or again:

> The honey of her Infant lips
> The bread and wine of her sweet smile,
> The wild game of her roving Eye
> Does him to Infancy beguile.

What has this, in all honesty, to do with Thomas Taylor's paraphrase of Plato's belief that the soul grows young as the body grows old? Rather, it is another glimpse from the vision of "Experience"; but set within a narrative so organized as to make that vision appear total, inter-locking through all its parts, and tragically inevitable.

[1] See above, p. 25.

Thus it is, I think, throughout the poem. The "aged Shadow", whose cottage is filled with treasure won from human suffering; the vagrants and travellers of whom it may be said

> *His grief* is their eternal joy;
> They make the walls and roof to ring

—the old man driven out like Lear; the vagrant, taken pity on, who becomes the oppressor (ll. 56–69); the lover "beguil'd . . . by various arts of Love & State"; the men who roam in the "desart" and flee in crazy terror at the birth of a child—all

> . . . such dreadful things
> As cold Earth wanderers never knew

are so described, of course, in irony. Cold Earth wanderers, Blake thought, know these things only too well. They are aspects of the world of everyday, as he now saw it, and they are shot through the poem in such a way that its over-riding impact is to come to seem an organizing and perspective of the here and the now. What the cyclic narrative does is something stressed and confirmed in the insistent rhythm of the poem, and the steely controlled weight of its superb monosyllabic lines, lines in which the innermost essence of the English language is realized and brought to fruition:

> To make it feel both cold and heat . . .

> And she grows young as he grows old . . .

> But She comes to the Man she loves,
> If young or old, or rich or poor . . .

> She nails him down upon the Rock,
> And all is done as I have told.

These things all come together to make the poem into a decisive, terrifying epitome of Blake's later vision of life. "Innocence" does not desert him entirely, but it finds little or no place in the later lyrics:

> . . . Tharmes brought his flock upon the hills, & in the Vales
> Around the Eternal Man's bright tent, the little Children play
> Among the woolly flocks. The hammer of Urthona sounds . . .
> The Sun arises from his dewy bed, & the fresh airs
> Play in his smiling beams . . .

But all this is now visionary in a new sense—it is the remote and chiliastic dream of regeneration that closes *The Four Zoas*. So far as the lyrics are concerned, Blake has brought his readers, in these latest poems, to the polar opposite of the state, and vision, of Innocence.

There is a certain kind of lyric poetry—perhaps the most essentially lyrical in kind—which appears to require some bond with popular poetry and with the traditional literary heritage of the common people, if it is to exist. After the medieval period, there seem to have been only three English poets who have achieved greatness in this way: Shakespeare whose link as a lyric poet is with the folk-song (though here there is much more to say, of course); Wordsworth whose was with the ballad in one of its kinds or another; and Blake who drew upon the wealth of the English Bible and the Protestant hymn. In Wordsworth's lyrical ballads there is sometimes a strangeness, a sense of the mysterious and uncomprehended, to which Blake's more decided mind seems to have been closed; but Blake was before Wordsworth, and his lyrical work has a fulness and variety, and also a whole-heartedness and absence of the reflective and diluted moralizing, which is not to be found in Wordsworth. He has come slowly to be seen for what he is; but it is now surely clear that it was he, more than any other poet of his period or just after, who recovered the lyric powers that had largely been lost between Traherne's time and his own. Moreover, Blake has only Hardy as something of a successor in English. Perhaps this is because England is now a country virtually without a rich literature of the common people such as it had in the past. Hardy aside, the only great poet of a kind comparable to Blake has been Yeats, whose work belongs to another country where popular culture still held the place it lost in our own.

But lyricism such as Blake's is not a technical success. It arises out of a certain sense—buoyant, joyous and yet serene—of life itself; and of course, from one point of view, the lyric product of that sense of life veritably constitutes what it embodies. It is this sense of life which I value most of all in Blake, and why I should therefore put *Songs of Innocence*, as a whole, above *Songs of Experience*. There is another point of view, though, and its strength shouts to be seen. Blake not only had that vision; he smarted under a searing awareness of how the great ones of the world rejected it or never glimpsed it. As a result, despite how the cruel time he lived in stifled his work, he is incomparably our most important poet of social and political comment. Here again, he has had

(this point was adverted to earlier on) no real followers: and our literature, and our present resources for writing, are lamentably the poorer
for that fact. On all these counts, Blake's value and importance are such
that they warrant the highest praise. It is not easy to think of a half-
dozen English poets whose work is more precious than his: or of many
more than that, who are his equals.

In Golden Square, there is nothing to commemorate Blake. Of all
things, the central place is occupied by a statue of George II. Nothing
could have a sharper irony, or more confirm what he himself thought of
the Powers That Be or what the English cultural scene has for so long
been like. But on my last visit there, I found something else as well:

> Cockle shells,
> Wedding bells,
> Evie, ivy, evoe (!)
> Mother's in the kitchen
> Doing her knitting,
> How many stitches can she do . . .?
> Five, ten, fifteen, twenty . . .

and so on. This was what the children sang as they played a skipping
game. One of them was what Blake would have called 'A Little Black
Girl'. Blake's memorial was a living one, and better than the king's.

Bibliography

Publication on Blake is exceedingly voluminous. This list merely mentions a small number of books and articles which I have found helpful in writing the present work, and which might not be noted by those who refer to fuller lists for guidance.

I. TEXTS

(a) Printed

The Complete Writings of William Blake, ed. Geoffrey Keynes. 1966. Brief, illuminating notes.

Selected Poems of William Blake, ed. F. W. Bateson. 1957. Full Introduction and notes.

William Blake, ed. Pinto, V. de Sola. 1965. Selections, with notes.

(b) Reproductions of Blake's Illuminated Texts

Songs of Innocence and of Experience, Henry Young & Sons. 1923. Monochrome etchings on Blake's own methods and after his designs.

Songs of Innocence, facsimile from a copy in the British Museum. Frederick Hollyer, 1923. An early facsimile, but not without quality and interest.

Songs of Innocence, facsimile from a British Museum copy. Ernest Benn, 1926. A clear, if diluted, coloured copy.

Songs of Experience, as the last entry, 1927. Blackish and less attractive.

Songs of Innocence and Experience, ed. Ruthven Todd. 1947. Black and white facsimile of a copy in the Houghton Library, Harvard. A fair general impression, save for colour, but useless for details. Brief foreword.

Songs of Innocence, facsimile of a copy in the Rosenwald Collection, Library of Congress. Trianon Press, 1954. Somewhat blurred, but in colour.

Songs of Innocence and Experience. As the last entry; original more richly coloured, so reproduction on the whole better. 1955.

See also Wicksteed, J. H., below.

II. BLAKE'S CONTEMPORARIES AND PREDECESSORS

Barbauld, Mrs. Anne Laetitia, *Hymns in Prose for Children*. 1782.
— *Lessons for Children*. 1787.
— *Poems*. 1773.
Bunyan, John, *A Book for Boys and Girls*. 1686 (9th edn, 1724, and thereafter entitled *Divine Emblems*).
Doddridge, Philip, *Works*. 10 Vols, 1803. Hymns, Vol. III.
Durfey, Thomas, *War and Mirth: or Pills to Purge Melancholy*. 3 Vols, 1719–20.
Fordyce, James, *Poems*. 1786.
Keate, George, *Poetical Works*. 2 Vols, 1781.
Pratt, Samuel, *Landscapes in Verse, Taken in Spring*. 1788.
Smart, Christopher, *Hymns for the Amusement of Children*. 1775.
Wesley, John, *Hymns for Children*. 1763.

III. HISTORICAL

Annual Register, *Passim*, but see especially 1794, Chap. XIV.
Cole, G. D. H., *Persons and Periods: Studies* (Chap. 6: 'A Study in Legal Repression').
Cole, G. D. H., and Postgate, R., *The Common People, 1746–1938*.
Lecky, William E. H. *A History of England in the Eighteenth Century*. 8 Vols. 1878.
Thompson, E. P., *The Making of the English Working Class*. 1963.
Williams, Basil, The Whig Supremacy. 1939 (Oxford History of England).
See also 28 Geo. III. c. 48. *An Act for the Better Regulation of Chimney Sweeps and their Apprentices*.

IV. BLAKE STUDIES, ETC.

Bett, H., *The Hymns of Methodism*. 3rd edn, 1945.
Bronowski, J., *William Blake: A Study*. 1944. Enlarged edn, 1955.
Davis, A. P., *Isaac Watts, his Life and Work*. New York, 1943.
Erdman, David V., *Blake: Prophet Against Empire*. 1954.
Escott, H., *Isaac Watts, Hymnographer*. 1962.
Gilchrist, Alexander, *Life of William Blake*, 1st edn, 1863, revised edn, 1945, by Ruthven Todd.
Hirsch, E. D., *Innocence and Experience: an Introduction to Blake*. 1964.
Keynes, Sir Geoffrey, *Blake Studies*. 1949.

Keynes, G. L., *On Editing Blake*.

Lowery, M. R., *Windows of the Morning: A Critical Study of 'Poetical Sketches'*. Yale, 1940.

Morton, A. L., *The Everlasting Gospel* (Blake and the "Ranter" sects). 1958.

Northall, G. F., *English Folk-Rhymes*. 1892.

Wicksteed, Joseph H., *Blake's Innocence and Experience*. 1928. With reproductions (very mediocre) of the etchings in the *Songs*: four in colour.

Wilson, Mona, *The Life of William Blake*. rev. edn, 1948.

V. ARTICLES

Erdman, D. V., 'Blake's Early Swedenborgism: a 20th Century Legend'. *Comparative Philology*, 1953, p. 247.

Harper, G. M., 'The Source of Blake's "Ah, Sunflower!"'. *Modern Language Review*, 1953, p. 139.

Mabbott, T. O., 'Blake's "Tyger"'. *Notes and Queries*, Nov. 17th, 1945.

Partridge, E. (ed.) *Poetical Sketches*. pub. Scholartis Press, 1927. With an essay on Blake's metric by Jack Lindsay.

Pierce, F. E., 'Blake and Thomas Taylor'. *"PMLA"*, 1928, p. 1140.

Pinto, V. de Sola, 'Isaac Watts and William Blake'. *Review of English Studies*, 1944, p. 214.

Raine, Kathleen, 'A Traditional Language of Symbols'. *Listener*, October 9th, 1958, pp. 559–60.

Robson, W. W., 'Kidnapping Blake'. *Spectator*, December 6th, 1957. pp. 806–8: correspondence in subsequent weeks.

Schorer, M., 'Swedenborg and Blake'. *Modern Philology*, 1938.

Index

of Poems Discussed[1]

[1] Briefer references are omitted.